THE A-Z OF CURIOUS

NORFOLK

STRANGE STORIES OF MYSTERIES, CRIMES AND ECCENTRICS

T0333258

SARAH E. DOIG

Dedicated to the memory of my father, who
first introduced me to curious Norfolk.

First published 2023
Reprinted 2024

The History Press
97 St George's Place, Cheltenham,
Gloucestershire, GL50 3QB
www.thehistorypress.co.uk

British Library Cataloguing in Publication Data.
A catalogue record for this book is available from the British Library.

ISBN 978 1 80399 440 6

Typesetting and origination by The History Press
Printed by TJ Books Ltd, Padstow, Cornwall

MIX
Paper from
responsible sources
FSC
www.fsc.org   FSC® C013056

Introduction

My earliest memories of Norfolk are of family visits to West Acre, just north of Swaffham, to visit the ancestors ... in the churchyard! It was, and still is, a village largely untouched by the stampede of time. The old forge, where my great, great-grandfather and his father before him had toiled in the heat, still stands in its prominent position opposite the village pub. The former village school, where my great-grandmother and her siblings learned to read and write, sits looking over the community it once educated. The Church of All Saints, which witnessed countless baptisms, marriages and burials of my forebears, still welcomes the faithful on Sundays. I owe my ancestors a huge debt of gratitude for introducing me to the county of Norfolk.

There is no escaping the fact that Norfolk lacks hills and mountains. The county does, however, more than compensate for this in offering the visitor sandy heathland, fens and navigable waterways, dramatic cliffs, as well as wide, open skies. While seeming to be a landscape with little habitation, it is teeming with villages and market towns, as well as the majestic city of Norwich.

Behind all of this are the people and events that have shaped what Norfolk is today. In researching and writing *The A–Z of Curious Norfolk* I have, therefore, tried to get under the surface and root out the curious, eccentric and mysterious stories that enrich Norfolk's story. Inevitably, some of the tales I tell will be familiar to those who have grown up in the county, or who have spent a lot of time immersing themselves in its history.

I have drawn inspiration from many sources, including the plethora of books and articles already written on a wide range of aspects of Norfolk. Where I have used others' stories as a starting point, I have tried to add something new to these, as well as consulting original sources where possible to check the veracity of the information.

I am extremely grateful to Tony Scheuregger for taking all the new black and white photographs used throughout this book, as well as the colour photograph on the front cover. I thoroughly enjoyed our many photographic excursions to the furthest reaches of the county, which allowed me to breathe the Norfolk air and soak up the atmosphere. Thank you also to Tony – a long-time Norwich resident – for the initial brainstorming sessions that helped shape the book. I am also indebted to Jonathan Plunkett for allowing me to use a number of black and white photographs taken by his late father, George Plunkett. I have also made use of some much older images, for which every attempt has been made to establish a copyright holder. However, if I have inadvertently used copyright material without permission, I apologise and will make the necessary correction at the first opportunity.

Finally, I simply could not have completed this book without the help and support of my husband, Mike. He has cooked, cleaned and washed, as well as mopped my fevered brow while pouring me a glass or two of wine. Mike has also, yet again, provided first-class, critical proofreading skills.

The author and her younger sister visiting their ancestors in West Acre churchyard. (Michael Booker)

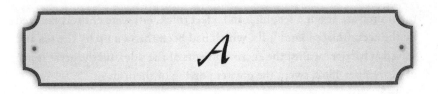

ABANDONED

The county of Norfolk seems to be crammed full of abandoned villages and communities (between 150 and 200 of them at last count) if this is not an oxymoron! The decline and desertion of villages across the county started in the mid-1400s and continued over the following few centuries.

The reasons for the disappearance of whole parishes from the county map are many and varied. It is often thought that many of Norfolk's villages were abandoned at the time of the Black Death in the mid-fourteenth century, when the plague decimated the population countrywide. The only likely candidate for this in our county is Little Ringstead. Many more parishes in Norfolk, however, were lost as a result of so-called emparking, such as Wolterton. Residents of this village, who lived just to the north of St Margaret's Church, were relocated as part of a redesign of Wolterton Hall and its estate in the eighteenth century, which took over the small community's land and houses.

Coastal erosion has been impacting communities in Norfolk for centuries and the resulting loss of villages, literally under the waves, has been felt not only on the north coast but also in the east, including the parishes of Keswick, Little Waxham and Whimpwell. One of the best-known victims of the sea in the north was Eccles-by-the-Sea, which was described in White's *History, Gazetteer and Directory of Norfolk 1883* as:

> a decayed parish, once a noted fishing town, but so wasted by the incursions of the ocean, that the inhabitants, in their petition for a reduction of taxes, in 1605, complained that they had then only 14 houses, and 300 acres of land, 'the rest being all destroyed by the sea, together with the church'. It had only 17 inhabitants in 1881, and comprises 253 acres of land divided into two farms. Eccles church was destroyed about 300 years ago; but the tower and part of the walls are still standing. The tower is round at the base and octagonal above, and is about 9 feet in diameter. The remains of the walls of

the church are about 6 feet high and 3 feet thick, but were entirely covered by the accumulated sand hills, which had been thrown up by the sea and served as barriers against the encroachments of the tides, till the great storm of November 1862, swept the greater portion of them away.

Eccles church tower stood until 1895, when it finally succumbed to the North Sea.

The desertion of some Norfolk villages has been more recent, and the abandonment by their communities has not been voluntary. The Thetford Forest area had been used by tanks in the First World War but in 1942, during the Second World War, the War Office decided that a battle-training area was required. It therefore evacuated an expanse in the south-west of the county, including the entire villages of Buckenham Tofts, Langford, Stanford, Sturston, Tottington and West Tofts, and rehoused its residents, telling them that they would be able to return after the conflict. The area, known as the Stanford Training Area (STANTA), was used extensively to prepare for the invasion of Normandy. The 7th Armoured Tank Division, nicknamed the Desert Rats, were stationed there from January to May 1944 to prepare for D-Day. After the war, the area continued to be used for military exercises and the villagers were never given the opportunity to return.

The ruined round tower of Thorpe Parva Church is all that is left of this deserted village. (Tony Scheuregger)

STANTA was famously used in the filming of many episodes of the television comedy series *Dad's Army*, including the closing credits where Captain Mainwaring is leading his men through a glade of Scots pine. More recently, in 2009, a complete replica Afghan village was constructed at a cost of £14 million. It was used to prepare troops for deployment to Afghanistan during that conflict and was populated by Afghan nationals, ex-Gurkha soldiers and amputee actors who simulated the Afghan National Army, locals and wounded soldiers. Every small detail of an authentic village was recreated, including a market with the smells of Afghan cooking and a mosque from which emanated calls to prayer.

Today, civilians can visit STANTA only as part of limited organised tours. Those who are lucky enough to do so can find the original pattern of country lanes, hedgerows and woods largely untouched. There are also four churches in the training area, maintained by the Ministry of Defence, but apart from an annual carol service in West Tofts for descendants of those villagers who once lived there, the ancient places of worship are silent.

★★★

By the end of the Second World War, Norfolk had no fewer than thirty-seven major military airfields. The county found itself in the forefront of the air war offensive, primarily because of its proximity to Continental Europe and, of course, due to its flat landscape, which lent itself to the speedy creation of runways. The RAF's Bomber Command operated out of Norfolk, as did the US 8th Army Air Force.

A few have survived as operational airfields, used either by the RAF or by private flying clubs, and the former US bomber base at Horsham St Faith is now Norwich International Airport! The rest, in various states of repair or disrepair, are commonly referred to as ghost fields. Sometimes, though, this can be a rather accurate description.

RAF Bircham Newton, just south of Docking, had first been used for military operations in the First World War and then, in the 1940s, it was redeveloped for use by RAF Coastal Command, which flew types such as the Lockheed Hudson light bomber and coastal reconnaissance plane. Visitors to the site in recent years have reported hearing ghostly noises of airfield life, as well as sounds of aircraft flying overhead. Some have even heard doors mysteriously closing and a ball being hit against the walls of the former squash courts. It is believed that three crewmen who crashed

Seething was one of Norfolk's airfields that was specifically constructed for the US 8th Army Air Force and the control tower is now a museum. (Tony Scheuregger)

their plane at the base, and who were keen players of the racquet sport, now haunt the courts at Bircham Newton.

At RAF Thorpe Abbotts, just east of Diss, the control tower was restored in the 1970s and now houses the 100th Bomb Group Memorial Museum, which is dedicated to US soldiers and members of the US 8th Army Air Force. The tower appears to have a friendly ghost who has been there for many decades.

Visitors to the museum have reported hearing noise of aircraft and radio 'chatter', as well as glimpses of a man dressed in flying gear. Sometimes he is seen standing at one of the upstairs windows at night. But it seems that Eddie, as the ghost is known, first appeared to US servicemen in early 1944, when he was seen walking through their quarters.

Stories of this ghost persisted and many of the airmen seemed spooked by it; so much so that the base commander banned all mention of Eddie under threat of court martial. Eddie is believed to be the spiritual manifestation of one of the pilots who died in 'Black Week' in October 1943 when the 100th Bomb Group suffered a large number of casualties and was almost entirely wiped out.

ANGELS

Slap bang in the middle of the Norfolk countryside, a few miles from Aylsham, stands one of the most eccentric churches, wholly designed by an equally eccentric Victorian clergyman. In fact, Edwin Lutyens, the distinguished architect, said the church was 'very naughty but built in the right spirit'.

Reverend Whitwell Elwin, a descendant of John Rolfe and his wife, the Native American woman, Pocahontas, was Rector of Booton from 1849 until his death in 1900. Not content with preaching in a rather 'bland' medieval parish church, he encased it in a fantastical Gothic creation of his own choosing, borrowing elements from various other places of worship.

The west doorway was inspired by a door at Glastonbury Abbey, the trefoil window above the chancel arch may have been copied from Lichfield Cathedral, and the hammerbeam roof, resplendent with angels, is said to have been based on that of St Botolph's Church in Trunch, also in Norfolk. The exterior of the Church of St Michael the Archangel in Booton is quite remarkable, with two slender towers at the west end, set diagonally to the main structure with a minaret-looking pinnacle in between.

The undoubted stars of the show inside are the host of angelic musicians depicted playing various instruments of the Bible, such as the harp and cymbals, as well as those from the Middle Ages like the vielle (or medieval fiddle) and the psaltery. Other angels are singing or reading and are shown in the company of saints and other female figures holding flowers. If you look closely, it is obvious that many of the girls' and angels' faces must have been drawn from real life. It is thought that they are portraits of 'Blessed Girls', as Reverend Elwin called his succession of young female friends and to whom the clergyman was, as the very diplomatic guidebook used to say, 'the affectionate, almost intimate, counsellor'.

★★★

Of the almost 170 medieval angel roofs that survive in England and Wales, Suffolk boasts the largest number, closely followed by Norfolk. These angels are to be found in parish churches high above our heads and all were constructed in the fifteenth and early sixteenth centuries.

Before Henry VIII broke with Rome in the 1530s, our churches were filled with carved and brightly coloured images ranging from rood screens with Christ and the saints to vivid wall paintings and stained glass depicting Biblical scenes. While many of these were destroyed, defaced or whitewashed over either during the English Reformation or in the Puritan purge a century later, many of the stunning carved-angel roofs survived, merely because they were out of reach.

These heavenly angels are often depicted playing musical instruments, such as at St Nicholas' Chapel in King's Lynn. Featured here are two lutes, a psaltery, a tabor, a rebec and a recorder. At Burlingham St Andrew there is a wonderful painted angel playing one of the louder instruments of the Middle Ages, the shawm.

Norfolk goes one better than Suffolk, and in fact the rest of the country, when it comes to stained glass featuring medieval musical angels. Examples pop up in churches across the county, including in East Barsham (where there are angels playing a shawm and a harp), Ketteringham and Shelton.

It is believed that the angel musicians, which often appear in the top part of the windows, as at Shelton where they can be seen to be playing instruments including a portative organ and a vielle, represent a heavenly presence over the characters depicted below. They demonstrate the importance of music as part of medieval worship.

A visitor to Norfolk's medieval churches should beware, though; not all the musicians are angels. At St Peter's in Ringland, near Norwich, there is a delightful, fourteenth-century roundel with a beautiful depiction of a centaur – a half-man, half-horse – with a forked, vine-leafed tail, playing a vielle!

This unusual fourteenth-century roundel is one of several delightful medieval treasures in Ringland Church. (Tony Scheuregger)

BARDS

Remarkably, there are two surviving medieval guildhalls in King's Lynn; the Guildhall of the Holy and Undivided Trinity, which is now the headquarters of the King's Lynn & West Norfolk Borough Council, and the Guildhall of St George. St George's Guildhall, currently owned by the National Trust, but leased and managed by the local borough council, is the oldest and largest complete medieval guildhall in England. It also boasts a long history of theatre production, with the earliest recorded play having been performed there in January 1445.

Recent academic research has backed up long-held claims that William Shakespeare played here with the Earl of Pembroke's Men in 1593 when the London theatres were closed due to the plague. One of Shakespeare's leading comic actors and a major influence on the bard's writing, Robert Armin, was born in King's Lynn. He was the first Feste in *Twelfth Night*, the Fool in *King Lear* and Autolycus in *A Winter's Tale*.

Other men from Norfolk are themselves immortalised in Shakespeare's plays. Sir Thomas Erpingham is a minor character in *Henry V*, where he lends the king his cloak with which to disguise himself, and he is mentioned (but does not appear) in *Richard II*. Sir Thomas served three generations of the House of Lancaster and had a military career that spanned four decades. In 1415, at around the age of 60, Erpingham was in command of the archers at the Battle of Agincourt at which the English under Henry V defeated the French.

In later life, the knight was a significant benefactor to the city of Norwich, funding the rebuilding of the Church of the Blackfriars (now known as St Andrew's Hall and Blackfriars' Hall or the Halls) following a devastating fire. In 1420, he also had the so-called Erpingham Gate constructed, which stands opposite the west door of Norwich Cathedral giving access into the Cathedral Close. The gate's style matches the west front of the cathedral and bears the family coat of arms. It also features a small statue of

Sir Thomas, which is thought to have been located originally on his tomb in the cathedral and placed on the gate in the seventeenth century.

Sir John Falstaff appears or is mentioned in no fewer than four plays by William Shakespeare. In both of the Bard of Avon's plays about Henry IV, Falstaff is a companion of Prince Hal, the future Henry V. Here, and in *The Merry Wives of Windsor*, Falstaff is primarily a comic figure; a fat, vain, cowardly knight who spends his time drinking and living on borrowed or stolen money.

This character's name almost certainly derives from the real-life Norfolk landowner Sir John Fastolf, and although there are said to be some comparisons in the real and fictional knights' lives, scholars believe that Falstaff's character is an amalgamation of several people with whose lives Shakespeare would have been familiar. That said, Sir John Fastolf, who lived at Caister Hall (later Caister Castle), was a soldier who served in the Hundred Years' War and during which he was accused of cowardice, having previously been recognised as a loyal and distinguished military man. In *Henry IV, Part I*, Falstaff delivers the now-famous phrase, 'The better part of valour is discretion'.

★★★

The life and achievements of one farmer from Little Dunham near Swaffham would have gone completely unnoticed by anyone other than his family, and perhaps his descendants, had it not been for a chance find. Even then, had it not been for the determination of the discoverer of this real gem to publish an account of her find in the *East Anglian Magazine*, we would still be none the wiser.

The parish register entries, census returns and electoral registers for Little Dunham allow us to flesh out the bare bones of Thomas Thompson's life. He was born in 1813 into a labouring family and by 1841 he was a shepherd. Thomas became a tenant farmer, farming some 11 acres.

It is a small entry in the *Lynn Advertiser* of 29 September 1883 that provides just a bit more colour to his story. This is an auction notice for all live and dead farming stock, as well as the household furniture, of Thompson who, the advert says, 'is leaving the county'.

So, where did Thomas go? Well, this is where the discovery of part of a printed poetry anthology by Thomas Thompson comes in. At the back of this volume is an illuminating biographical snippet that begins, 'The

Author of these verses at the age of 70 left his native village, Dunham in Norfolk, for Tasmania on a visit to his children December 10th 1883, and arrived in a sailing vessel on the 4th April of the following year.' It continues with details of his return to England, as well as dates of a further voyage to Tasmania, finally returning to this country in May 1891. It is probable that despite his assertion that 'he contemplates going out again', he was, sadly, never to make a third visit to his family; his burial is recorded in Little Dunham in 1896.

It is Thomas Thompson's poems, though, that give us an insight into the farmer's soul, including his mixed feelings at leaving his home village for Australia, for he writes:

> Farewell to old England I am going from home,
> I'm going to leave you and going from home;
> I'm going across the salt sea for to roam,
> Far far from old England, far away from my home.
>
> Farewell peaceful cottage, farewell happy home,
> Where I once was so happy, so happy at home;
> But friends have forsook me and caused me to roam,
> So I never more shall be happy at home.
>
> Farewell, Little Dunham, the place of my birth,
> For of all other places tis thee I love best;
> I'd a few friends in Dunham, I once loved sincere,
> But they most have forsook me, so I could not stay there.

BATS

The Paston family of north Norfolk are best known for the surviving collection of letters dating from the fifteenth century, written to and by family members. They provide historians with an amazingly detailed insight into many aspects of upper-class life in medieval England.

The Pastons rose from humble origins into one of the four largest landowners in the country during the Tudor era. One member of this great family who used his wealth to the benefit of others was Sir William Paston, who established a Free Grammar School in North Walsham. He also

Paston's sixteenth-century Great Barn offers a haven for wildlife today. (George Plunkett)

founded the almshouses in the village of Paston, where he lived in Paston Hall. Although the hall has long since disappeared from the landscape, the nearby thatched Great Barn, built by Sir William in 1581 as a grain store and threshing barn, still stands and is the only complete building remaining from the Paston Estate. It is a grand building, approximately 70m long and 16m high and has been designated a Grade II listed building by English Heritage due to its architectural and historical importance.

Over the centuries, the Great Barn has played host to many farm animals but today it is home to one of the few colonies of barbastelle bats in the country. The barbastelle is distinguishable by its short, upturned nose and has long, silky blackish-brown fur. The scientific name *Barbastella* comes from the Latin for 'star beard' and refers to the white tips on the bat's fur.

Although there are a handful of other colonies of barbastelle bats in England, the Paston colony are the only ones who roost in a building, the others being in trees. The barbastelles mostly roost in the large crevices in the timber lintels over the barn doors.

Seven other species of bats have been recorded in and around the Great Barn, including the Nathusius' pipistrelle and Natterer's, as well as the common and soprano bat. Because of the protected status of the bats, the barn and the surrounding area has been designated a Biological Site of Scientific Interest, as well as a Special Area of Conservation. There is, understandably, no public access to the Great Barn, which is currently leased from the North Norfolk Historic Buildings Trust by English Nature.

★★★

Vice Admiral Horatio Nelson is, unarguably, Norfolk's most celebrated son. He was born into a relatively prosperous family in Burnham Thorpe, where he was the sixth of eleven children of the local rector. Nelson attended the grammar school in North Walsham founded by Sir William Paston, and then King Edward VI Grammar School in Norwich.

His highly successful naval career began at the age of 12 in 1771 and the young Horatio discovered that he suffered from seasickness, a complaint he experienced for the rest of his life. By 1793, Captain Nelson was on HMS *Agamemnon* and it was while in command of this sixty-four-gun ship, which battled the French Navy in Corsica, that he was struck in the right eye by debris. Many people mistakenly believe that he lost his eye completely but although he regained partial sight in his damaged eye, by his own account, Nelson could only 'distinguish light from dark but no object'.

Four years later, the newly promoted Rear Admiral Nelson fought against a Spanish fleet in the Battle of Santa Cruz de Tenerife, when his right arm was hit by a musket ball. The arm was so badly shattered that it had to be amputated.

A Nelson in cricket is a term applied to a score of 111 or its multiples (known as double Nelson, triple Nelson, etc.) and is thought to be extremely unlucky. One explanation of such a strange term for this cricketing superstition is that it refers to the one eye, one arm and one leg that Nelson is said to have lost. This is clearly not accurate, as he never lost a leg. Other sources quote the fact that the term applies to Nelson's three major naval victories (won, won, won). It is, however, more likely that 111 merely refers to the shape of the game's wicket without its bails and therefore clearly represents misfortune for the team batting.

★★★

Like many other Norfolk villages, Old Buckenham has its own cricket club, which fields several men's, women's and youth teams. However, in contrast to other village clubs in the county, Old Buckenham's ground has a rather distinguished past. It was created by a wealthy industrialist called Lionel Robinson as part of a larger expansion scheme at his home in Old Buckenham Hall. Robinson, who made his fortune as a stockbroker and financier during the mining boom in Australia and then on the London Stock Exchange, was known to entertain lavishly on his Norfolk estate, which he had purchased from Prince Frederick Duleep Singh in 1906.

As well as being a successful breeder and owner of racehorses, Lionel Robinson also enjoyed cricket. He reportedly used turf specially brought over from Australia to create the two pitches at Old Buckenham Hall and he employed former England captain Archie MacLaren as cricketing manager. Robinson's personal team went on to play several first-class cricket matches, including against the touring South Africans in 1912, Cambridge University in 1913 and Oxford University a year later.

In 1919, the first international cricket match played in England after the First World War was played at Old Buckenham, between the home team and the Australian Imperial Forces.

Lionel Robinson died of cancer at Old Buckenham Hall in 1922 but not before he had managed, in 1921, to attract the touring Australian test team to play a three-day game at his cricket ground against an almost full-strength England side playing as L.G. Robinson's XI.

BLACK

We could probably all have a stab at naming an author who wrote a one-hit wonder, where the writer has become well known on the strength of just one work. Norfolk has its own one-hit wonder of the literary world – and what a wonder it is, having sold over 50 million copies worldwide, as well as having had several film and television adaptations made.

The narrator of the book is not a human but a horse, the novel's full title page reading '*Black Beauty: His Grooms and Companions. The Autobiography of a Horse*. Translated from the original Equine by Anna Sewell.'

The author was born in Great Yarmouth in 1820 and, although her parents moved the family to London shortly afterwards, Anna Sewell and her brother were frequently sent to their grandparents' farm in Buxton, near Aylsham. It was here that she learnt to ride a horse. However, at the age of 14, Anna had a fall and severely injured her ankles. For the rest of her life, she could not walk very far or stand without using a crutch. She therefore used horse-drawn carriages to get around, which contributed to her love of the animals, as well as her concern for the humane treatment of horses.

Sewell's *Black Beauty* was her only published work, which, in fact, came out just five months before she died. Although it is usually considered to be a children's book, this was not her intention, more that she had a special aim to 'induce kindness, sympathy, and an understanding treatment of

Jarrolds flagship department store is now one of Norwich's well-known landmarks. (Tony Scheuregger)

horses'. It was the Norwich publisher Jarrolds who published *Black Beauty* on 24 November 1877, having paid Anna Sewell a single, one-off payment of £40. In 2015, Jarrolds produced a hardback reprint of the 1912 edition of the novel with colour illustrations by British artist Cecil Aldin.

★★★

The colour black is, of course, associated with mourning for a deceased loved one. Mourning crêpe (or crape) was the fabric of choice for clothes worn for this. The meaning of the word 'crape' is to curl or to crimp and the crimp in the wool was obtained by twirling the thread by hand before it was woven, causing the fabric to shrink in hot water.

Before the seventeenth century, mourning crape was made from wool, particularly worsted wool manufactured in Norfolk. Then in the early 1600s, Norwich manufacturers started making a lighter crape fabric using silk in the warp instead of wool. This was known as bombazine and, for many years, Norwich had an almost monopoly of this trade. By the 1800s, mourning crape was made entirely from silk.

A strict dress code for mourning has been observed from time to time over the centuries, never more so than in the formal Victorian era and, in particular, after the death of the queen's husband, Prince Albert, in 1861. Full mourning for a widow lasted a year and consisted of garments made of plain, matte-black fabrics, worn without jewellery. After a year, a widow could add trimmings and simple jewellery and could introduce grey and subtle shades of purple. Sadly, very few examples of mourning crape survive due, in part, to the fabric's fragility but also because it was believed that it was unlucky to keep it in the house after the mourning period was over.

By far the largest manufacturer of crape in Britain in the second half of the nineteenth century was Grout & Co., which employed over 3,000 workers in mills in Norwich, Great Yarmouth and Ditchingham. Joseph Grout, who founded the company in 1806 at Patterson's Yard, Magdalen Street in Norwich, was descended from Huguenot refugees from the Low Countries. He started to manufacture Norwich Crape, also known as *Crêpe Anglais*, which was perhaps the most intricate and difficult of all textile fabrics to produce. His raw silk came from Bengal, China and Italy.

The embossed effect was obtained by passing the fabric between two heated rollers. One of these was metal that had been engraved by hand with the required design. The other roller was made of compressed paper. Before they were ready for use on the fabric, both rollers were run together under pressure so that the pattern on the metal roller had been transferred to the paper one. Such was Grout's success that others established crape mills in Norwich.

In the early part of the twentieth century, the custom of wearing mourning crape began to decline and the industry suffered a severe blow when, on the death of Edward VII, it was ordered that crape was not to be worn for court mourning. The three remaining manufacturers at that time – Grouts, Hindes of Norwich and Courtaulds of Essex – turned their attention to the manufacture of silk for everyday dresses instead.

★★★

In May 1967, the Beatles released their eighth studio album *Sgt. Pepper's Lonely Hearts Club Band* and ever since it has topped music critics' and listeners' polls as the best album of all time. One of the tracks on this album that makes use of innovations such as sound effects and tape manipulation is 'Being for the Benefit of Mr. Kite!' John Lennon drew inspiration for the song from a nineteenth-century circus poster for Pablo Fanque's Circus Royal, which he bought in an antiques shop and the lyrics detail the evening circus programme, which concluded with Henry the Horse dancing a waltz. This song was banned from being played on the BBC, apparently because the phrase 'Henry the Horse' combined two words known as slang for heroin. Lennon denied any link with this banned substance, although he is believed to have said, 'Everything from the song is from that poster except the horse wasn't called Henry'.

Pablo Fanque was, in fact, the first black circus proprietor in Britain and was born in Norwich in 1810 as William Darby. At around the age of 10, on the death of his father, William was apprenticed to a circus run by William Batty and there he learned rope-dancing and tumbling, as well as becoming a talented equestrian performer.

His first public performance in Norwich was on Boxing Day in 1821, when he was billed as Young Darby. By 1828, the same man was performing under the name Young Pablo at a show at the Norwich Pantheon and in 1840, when William Batty's circus again performed in Norwich, the name Pablo Fanque appears.

At Fanque's debut in London in 1847, *The Illustrated London News* reported, 'Mr. Pablo Fanque was the hit of the evening. The steed in question was Beda, the black mare that Fanque had bought from Batty. That the horse attracted so much attention was testament to Fanque's extraordinary horse training skills.'

The nineteenth-century poster that inspired John Lennon.

Pablo Fanque eventually established a circus of his own and over a period of thirty years, his circus toured the country and he was considered one of the top performers in the profession. After his death, the chaplain of the Showmen's Guild of Great Britain wrote, 'In the great brotherhood of the equestrian world there is no colour line [bar], for, although Pablo Fanque was of African extraction, he speedily made his way to the top of his profession. The camaraderie of the ring has but one test – ability.'

★★★

In the Middle Ages, Thetford had been an important ecclesiastical centre, with five religious houses, twenty churches and several monastic hospitals. The Dissolution of the Monasteries all but knelled the death bell for the town's economy: its revenue from the religious institutions, and from the pilgrims they attracted, had disappeared. However, the town had been successful in obtaining a royal charter in 1574 and from that time was governed independently from the Crown by a formally constituted corporation. Even before this, the town had had a right to appoint its own mayor since 1199. It is perhaps fitting, then, that Thetford should be able to boast of having appointed the first ever black mayor in any British town.

Allan Glaisyer Minns was born in the Bahamas in 1858 and, after studying at Nassau Grammar School, moved to England to train to become a doctor at Guy's Hospital in London. He was registered with the British Medical Association in 1884 and moved to Thetford to practise as a GP. His eldest brother, Pembroke, had already established himself as a doctor in the town, becoming physician to the Thetford Cottage Hospital. Allan, too, played an important part in the life of the community, serving as medical officer to the workhouse.

In the early 1900s, Minns published several articles in the *Thetford and Watton Times*, exhorting people to get as much fresh air and exercise as they could. In 1903, Minns was elected to Thetford Borough Council and one year later, he was elected as mayor, a position he held for two years. For many years, it was believed that John Archer, who was Mayor of Battersea in 1913, was the first black British mayor, but the history books have now been rewritten to celebrate the achievements of Allan Glaisyer Minns.

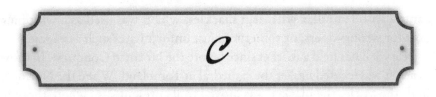

C

CROSS

In the 1720s, the writer Daniel Defoe visited East Anglia and observed:

> Between the frontiers of Suffolk and the city of Norwich [...] are the
> following market-towns, viz:– Thetford, Hingham, Harleston, Diss,
> West Dereham, E. Dereham, Harling, Attleborough, Watton, Bucknam,
> Windham, Loddon, etc. Most of these towns are very populous and large;
> but that which is most remarkable is, that the whole country round them
> is so interspersed with villages, and those villages so large, and so full of
> people, that they are equal to market-towns in other countries; in a word,
> they render this eastern part of Norfolk exceeding full of inhabitants.

For many centuries before Defoe visited, markets and the marketplace were the focal points for the population from the town itself and the surrounding rural area. It was where they met to trade, buy and sell fresh produce, assemble for celebrations and to hear proclamations of national events. Petty criminals, including those tradesmen who sold inferior goods, were regularly punished with the humiliation of being put in the stocks or the pillory for a few hours. These would have stood close by the market cross, which was at the very heart of the marketplace. Indeed, New Buckenham's surviving market cross still retains, in its open lower floor, a

The whipping post at Bintree is thankfully not used today to punish locals. (George Plunkett)

central wooden pillar with arm shackles, which was used as a whipping post for wrong-doers, or sometimes just unfortunates such as vagrants.

Norwich has held a market since before the Norman Conquest. In those times, it was located nearer the cathedral in Tombland. When the Normans built the castle, the market was moved to its present site, where those in the castle could keep a closer eye on commercial transactions. A wooden market cross was built there in the time of Edward III to mark the fact that the king had granted the city the formal right to hold a market.

In 1502, a grander, replacement market cross was commissioned. This was an impressive stone structure some 20m high, which sat on an octagonal plinth 10m in diameter. We know from surviving Court Books and governing Assembly Minute Books that Norwich's market cross was at the centre of the ceremonies to welcome Elizabeth I to the city in August 1578. The records reveal that the market cross was to be repainted 'tymber colour' and white, and the public pillory and cage were removed from the marketplace to a more distant location, ensuring miscreants did not escape punishment just because of the royal visit!

Sadly, in 1732, the market cross was deemed too expensive to maintain and so it was dismantled and the stone sold for £125. In 2005, during renovation work on the present-day market stalls, archaeologists surveying the site revealed the foundations of this cross. Its footprint is now marked in a red outline embedded in the flooring of the market.

Sadly, many other market crosses have disappeared completely from Norfolk towns. In July 1836, Great Yarmouth's local newspaper reported:

On Friday last the market cross was sold by public tender for £55 6s and on Monday morning workmen commenced pulling it down. It has now entirely disappeared to the gratification of the residents in the marketplace to whom it had long been a great annoyance in consequence of its having become a rendezvous for the dissolute. Some people lament the loss of such an old building but the corporation removed it as a public nuisance which although at some time in the past have been useful but has long since ceased to be so and has fallen to abuse and rottenness.

Thus, a building that had existed, in some form or other, since the fourteenth century ceased to be.

As was the case in Norwich, we know that a market cross was erected on a site where permission had been granted, usually by a monarch or bishop,

The market cross at Wymondham is still a meeting place for residents.
(Tony Scheuregger)

to hold a regular fair or market. These crosses took many forms: some were simple carved wooden spires, but others, like in Norfolk's capital, were more elaborate, ornate covered buildings.

One of the county's most impressive surviving market crosses is in Wymondham. It is a wooden structure that was built at a cost of £25 after the Great Fire of Wymondham in 1615, to replace an earlier cross. Over the centuries, the town's market cross has served many purposes. At the end of the nineteenth century and into the early twentieth century, it served as a subscription reading room and, for a short time in the 1930s, it housed a public library. Since 1990, the cross has been home to the Wymondham Tourist Information Centre.

CUSTOMS

Herring fishing has always been a vital part of Great Yarmouth's economy. Over the centuries, it has provided employment for fishermen and a wide range of related trades, such as salting and curing of the herring and boatbuilding. Indeed, the town's coat of arms features three lions with herring tails.

Herring was one of the main staple foods in medieval England and the Great Yarmouth Assembly closely regulated and protected the industry, resulting in it being the fourth-richest settlement in the country. To encourage outsiders to buy Yarmouth herring, the town traditionally held an annual herring fair for forty days, between Michaelmas (29 September) and Martinmas (10 November).

Before the Reformation, Great Yarmouth's fishing nets were blessed by churchmen and a tradition of 'wetting of the nets' took place on the seashore, although this custom gradually fell away, until it was revived by the Victorians. After a further gap of several years, the tradition of blessing the nets was recreated again in 2010.

Nowadays, St Nicholas Church, otherwise known as Great Yarmouth Minster, plays host to a blessing of the nets service every October. The church is decorated with fishing nets and a customary supper follows the ceremony with – yes, you've guessed it – herring on the menu!

***

Among the treasures to be found inside the parish church at Heydon, a picturesque village not far from Aylsham, are a surviving series of medieval wall paintings, a fifteenth-century wooden, painted rood screen, separating the main body of the church from the chancel – where the priests historically presided over the services – and a 500-year-old font.

Another slightly more unusual feature is an agricultural plough. Although a rare sight in Norfolk churches, it is by no means the only such example. This plough bears witness to a custom that dates back far beyond the origins of Heydon's church, and indeed any other in the county.

Although written references to Plough Monday date back to the Tudor era, it is thought that this designation, and the traditions surrounding it, originate with the pagan Nordic people who invaded England in the Dark Ages. Plough Monday is celebrated on the first Monday after Twelfth Night and is traditionally the day when the farmworkers returned to their work to till the soil after the Christmas holiday. In the Middle Ages, these ploughboys, who were seasonal workers, would disguise themselves and go around to the local wealthy householders begging for money.

This unusual artefact in Heydon's church reminds of the ancient custom of Plough Monday. (Tony Scheuregger)

By the 1400s, Plough Monday had become a Christian tradition where the day was dedicated to raising funds for the parish, which in turn supported the poor. Groups of skilled ploughmen formed plough guilds, which kept a 'plough light' – a candle – alight in the church all year round and their ploughs were often brought into the church to be blessed by the priest.

When Henry VIII broke with the Roman Catholic church and declared himself head of the new Church of England, plough guilds and their customs were banned. But the Reformation did not end the Plough Monday and its activities altogether.

In the seventeenth century, the tradition was revived within the community, this time as a secular occasion. The customs observed on this day varied from region to region, but a common feature was for a decorated plough to be dragged through the neighbourhood, accompanied by musicians and dancers, with money being collected from residents. Rather than earlier collections for maintenance of the 'plough light' in the local church, the money was now spent in the local alehouse! In Norfolk, Plough Pudding, a boiled suet pudding containing meat and onions, was also traditionally eaten on this day.

★★★

While some customs, like Plough Monday, are to be found across the country, albeit with regional variations, there is one tradition that seems to be unique to Norfolk and, to some extent, Norwich in particular. It is linked to the celebration known the world over as Valentine's Day and this is where, in Norfolk, Jack Valentine makes an appearance.

To be precise, Jack Valentine appears on Valentine's Eve, 13 February, under cover of darkness. He knocks on a front door and leaves a present for the household, traditionally a home-made one, on the doorstep. However, before the door is opened, Jack has disappeared.

In some iterations of the custom, Jack Valentine tows the gift wrapped in newspaper down the garden path, attached to a piece of string. Nobody knows how old this Norfolk custom is, although it certainly goes back at least 200 years. In the nineteenth century, a variation on the Jack Valentine tradition was enacted, where the local children would go out before dawn on 14 February singing rhymes in exchange for sweets and gifts. One such verse goes:

> Good morrow Valentine,
> God bless the baker,
> You'll be the giver,
> And I'll be the taker.

Although nowadays, Jack Valentine's presents are mostly shop bought, the custom is kept alive by Norfolk-bred folk across the globe.

DEMONS

The coast of Norfolk stretches for nearly 100 miles from the Wash in the west to Hopton-on-Sea, south of Great Yarmouth. The coastline itself is abundant with flora and fauna, including the seal colonies and birdlife for which the county is famous. In fact, three quarters of the north Norfolk coastline is designated an Area of Outstanding Natural Beauty.

However, the same coastline has proved extremely hazardous to ships for centuries. For example, in the early 1800s it was estimated that four fifths of all shipwrecks in the UK were off the coasts of Norfolk and Suffolk. There is a series of sandbanks in the North Sea that run from Cromer to Happisburgh and are known collectively as the Devil's Throat because of the regularity with which boats are swallowed up by the water, sending unwitting sailors to their deaths.

Legend has it that Devil's Alley in King's Lynn is so named after a demonic footprint left in anger by the Devil after he was driven away by a priest wielding holy water and prayers. Round the coast in Great Yarmouth, a rather strange object used to sit outside the Church of St Nicholas. The so-called Devil's Seat was made from the skull and vertebrae of a sperm whale that was washed ashore at Caister-on-Sea in 1582. It was said, then, to bring deadly disaster to anyone sitting on the chair. Oddly, though, when the seat was later moved to a niche by the west door of the church, it was said, instead, to bestow a rather unusual power. Whoever was faster – bride or groom – to sit in the seat after a marriage in the church would be destined to have all the power in the new home.

The Devil also ventured inland at various times in Norfolk's history. Devil's Ditch is a 2-mile-long dyke flanked by low banks that run north–south across Garboldisham Heath towards East Harling. According to folklore, the Devil made the ditch by dragging one of his hooves along the ground. When he scraped the dirt from his hoof, it flew into the air and landed in Thetford, thus forming the mound of Castle Hill. Today, it is the highest such castle mound in England, although no trace of the Norman castle remains. To the north-east of Castle Hill there is a water-filled hollow called Devil's Hole. Some say that if you walk around the hill seven times at midnight, the demon himself appears.

***

It takes a brave, or perhaps foolish, man to make a pact with the Devil with no intention of keeping his promises. Sir Berney Brograve inherited Waxham Hall in 1753 from his father, as well as several manors, including Sea Palling and Horsey. His income was dependent on farming the land but his low-lying fields along the coast were often hit by erosion and floods. In an attempt to regain land that had been taken over by seawater,

Sir Berney Brograve regretted making a pact with the Devil. (Tony Scheuregger)

Sir Berney built a windpump to drain water from the Brograve levels into the man-made Waxham New Cut. It was known locally as the Devil's Mill and some people believe that dark magic was practised there.

There is a story that persists that Sir Berney Brograve wagered his soul that he could out-mow the Devil over 2 acres of bean plants. The Devil easily won and therefore sought to collect Berney's soul. In an attempt to hide from the demon, Sir Berney hid in his mill. The Devil, who was unable to enter, beat furiously on the door with his hooves.

The next morning when the baronet emerged from hiding, he saw that the door of his windpump was covered in footprints and the tower had been rocked on its foundations by the Devil trying to blow the structure down. From then on, it has leaned towards the west. Some locals believe that Sir Berney Brograve was cursed by the Devil to wander forever on the land and his ghost now haunts the deserted and derelict mill.

DISS

There is a long-running game I have been playing with friends of mine, often on long car journeys to relieve boredom or over a glass or two of wine. It all started on a shopping trip to Diss when, along the high street, I encountered one of those shops selling all manner of household items at cheap prices and wondered whether they had missed a trick by not calling it 'Disscount'. This very quickly led to a whole raft of suggestions for other specialist retail outlets, as well as for all other buildings and establishments in the town. One of my all-time favourites is 'Dissgruntle', which would, naturally, be the local pork butcher. Then there is 'Dissplace', the estate agents, the church, 'Dissbelief', the spare limb manufacturers (or perhaps the gun shop) called 'Dissarm', 'Dissolve' the local private eye, as well as 'Disscover', the travel agents, and the office which is a tourist's first port of call, 'Dissinfomation'.

I was delighted to find an actual shop in the town that sells handmade and vintage items called 'Disstressed', but I remain somewhat Diss-appointed that others haven't jumped on the bandwagon. There are some places that have proved harder than others to find a name for, including the bookshop or library, until one of my nieces came up with 'Disslexia'!

Perhaps not unsurprisingly, I was not the first person to invent Diss puns. Thomas Edward Amyot was a medical doctor who established a practice in

Crown Street, Diss, in 1846. He was a keen amateur naturalist, astronomer and chess player. Amyot was also heavily involved in philanthropic work in the town and helped found the Diss Coffee Tavern.

Coffee houses or taverns sprung up in the second half of the nineteenth century as an alternative to the public houses hitherto frequented by men from the working class. Instead of drinking away their pay, and their families' livelihoods, in the alehouses, men could drink coffee, tea and cocoa in comfortable and relaxing surroundings. Daily and weekly newspapers were provided and gentle pursuits like card games were encouraged.

Shakespeare and other older literature were a particular passion of the doctor's, but it is his talent for writing that is his most enduring legacy due, in part, to the efforts of his friends. Two years after Thomas Amyot's death in 1895, they published an anthology of his written work, *Verses and Ballads*, as a memorial to him. It is here that his sense of humour shines through in several epitaphs he penned. One of these is a simple but witty two-line, entitled '(By a Sufferer) On … Esquire', which reads:

> He paid the debt of Nature and 'tis said
> This is the only debt he ever paid.

Another epitaph introduces us to Amyot's fondness for Diss puns under the heading 'At a Concert, in the Summer of 1894 our principal Singer failed to appear':

> Our Tenor cometh not, alack a-day!
> The even tenor of his way diverted;
> And we who go to concerts here at Diss,
> Of course you'll guess were somewhat dis-concerted.

Sadly, my favourite poem by him does not appear in the anthology. Instead, it is quoted in an *East Anglian Magazine* article about 'Thomas Amyot of Diss', but I have no doubt this is by him:

> To Diss a man was sent to live
> And there he trade began.
> And lived, though happy all his life,
> A Diss-appointed man.

Great country customers he had
And they were well supplied.
And as from Diss they missed his goods
They felt diss-satisfied.

The townsfolk all approved of him
As honest, kind and just.
And as they would have trusted him
They showed him much diss-trust.

At length the tender passion strong
Our grocer's bosom moved,
His friends approved his choice, and so
His choice was diss-approved.

To church he went with Betty Gibbs.
They joined in vow and prayer.
And lived, united many years,
A diss-united pair.

At length his evil day had come
As come to all it must.
The wind blew down a wall on him
And killed him with diss-gust.

His funeral to the cold grave came
And people have averred
That as they laid him in the ground
His corpse was diss-interred.

★★★

The 90 acres of Diss Common, or Moor, Diss-appeared over 200 years ago, when it was enclosed by Act of Parliament in 1816. Today, Victoria Road, with its garages, car showrooms, takeaway businesses, station and main railway line from Norwich to London stand on this former common ground.

Over the centuries, the common witnessed many unsavoury events. In 1742, Robert Carleton was executed here and then hung up in chains in a gibbet. Around 5,000 people turned out to see the man who had been found guilty of poisoning Mary Frost with mercury sublimate, which he had placed in her dinner of boiled mutton.

Since medieval times right through to its enclosure, Diss Common was also the place where the game of camping or camp ball was played. This was a primitive form of football-come-rugby and traditionally used an animal's bladder filled with dried peas as a ball. However, far from being the friendly but competitive game we know today, camping was described by an Elizabethan Puritan writer as 'a bloody murdering practice with everyone lying in wait for his adversary to pick him on the nose and dash him against the heart with his elbows'.

In fact, the name of this game is said to have been derived from the Anglo-Saxon word '*cempan*', meaning 'to fight' and, indeed, the players – usually between ten and twenty – were referred to as combatants. There were numerous versions of the rules (in the loosest sense of the word) of the game of camping but whether the teams were able to kick, carry or throw the ball through the goals or just allowed to run with the ball to score, a fixture never ended 'without black eyes, bloody noses, broken heads or shins, or other series mischiefs'.

It was on Diss Common that a truly legendary game of camping took place in the mid-eighteenth century between sides from Norfolk and Suffolk. According to oral accounts handed down, 600 players took part. The Norfolk men, brimming with confidence, are said to have asked their rivals, 'Have you brought your coffins?' At the end of fourteen hours, the Suffolk team won the match, which resulted in no fewer than nine men dying of injuries sustained during the game.

Despite the regular maimings and occasional death during such matches, the game continued to be played in Norfolk until 1831 when 'neither the camping nor the subsequent wrestling were well contested'.

DRAGONS

One of the many interesting exhibits in the Norwich Castle Museum is a dragon that dates from 1795. Not, you will be pleased to hear, a real, live, fire-breathing one, but one made from basketwork over which a painted canvas is stretched. It is affectionately known as Snap and, although this dragon is no longer in use, the ceremony for which it was made continues and its successors still make an appearance once a year in the streets of the city.

The dragon – or rather a person wearing the dragon costume – follows the town crier in a procession to mark the start of Norwich's civic year and the appointment of the new lord mayor of the city. Snap is accompanied around Norwich by men called the Whifflers, whose office was originally created to make a path through the crowds during processions of dignitaries.

The tradition of using a dragon in Norwich processions started in medieval times and although nowadays they are associated with civic events, they started life as part of religious ceremonies. The Guild of St George was founded in Norwich in 1385 and had religious, charitable and social purposes. The guild had a small chapel in the cathedral dedicated to St George and paid for a priest to say a daily mass there to pray for the welfare of its members.

On St George's Day – 23 April – the guild would process to the cathedral for a service that was followed by a grand banquet. It is highly likely that a dragon made an appearance at these early ceremonies, although it is not until 1480 that we find the following reference in the minutes of the guild assembly, 'The George shall go in procession and make conflict with the Dragon'.

It was in the fifteenth century that the Guild of St George took on secular, as well as religious, rights and it was linked to Norwich's civic administration. From 1585, the guild organised a combined St George's Day celebration with that of the installation of the new lord mayor and, naturally, Snap the Dragon played a key role in the festivities.

★★★

Many years ago the good people of Ludham were shocked by the appearance of a hideous monster. It was said to have resembled a dragon or monstrous lizard. It was covered with scales and had wings. Its frightful mouth was rendered formidable by tremendous teeth. It was supposed to measure from 12 to 15 feet in length.

So begins a note by William Henry Cooke of Stalham in the late nineteenth century. According to his account, he compiled this story using local history documents. Cooke had earned a living as a clerk to the school board and in later life described himself as a newspaper correspondent. He may, then, have had access to back copies of local newspapers. One such paper was the *Norfolk Chronicle*, which on 28 September 1782 published the following story:

> On Monday the 16th inst. a snake of enormous size was destroyed at Ludham, in this county, by Jasper Andrews, of that place. It measured five feet eight inches long, was almost three feet in circumference, and had a very long snout: what is remarkable, there were two excrescences on the fore part of the head which very much resembled horns. This creature seldom made its appearance in the daytime, but kept concealed in subterraneous retreats, several of which have been discovered in town; one near the tanning-office, another in the premises of the Rev. Mr. Jeffery, and another in the lands occupied by Mr. William Popple, at the Hall. The skin of the above surprising reptile is now in the possession of Mr J. Garrett, a wealthy farmer in the neighbourhood.

Dragons are surprisingly commonplace in Norfolk.

This rather startling story appears in a wonderful potpourri of 'Home News', sandwiched between a report of an escape of convicts from Chelmsford Gaol and news that the annual fair at Bury St Edmunds was getting under way. So perhaps such occurrences were commonplace in eighteenth-century England!

William Cooke must have done some more digging in the archives because his account is not only illustrated with a wonderful dragon drawing, recording that this was taken from an old manuscript, but he also gives far greater detail as follows:

As it was only visible after sunset, none dared to leave their houses when it was dark. It formed a large burrow which was known to extend from the yard at the back of the Carpenter's Arms just past the old school house. Every morning the exit was filled up with bricks and stones, and then as often, reopened at night by the monster. One bright sunshiny afternoon, to the horror of the inhabitants, it was seen to leave the burrow. As soon as it had got some distance away, a courageous parishioner dropped a single large round stone into the mouth of the burrow, completely filling it up. After basking in the sun for some time the monster returned. Not being able to remove the stone it turned away bellowing and lashing its sides furiously with its tail. It then made its way across the fields in the direction of the Bishop's Palace. Turning to the left it made its way along the dreary causeway leading to the ruined St Benets Abbey Gateway. Round and round it ran, throwing up stones and dirt in its fury and raising its hideous form up against the ruined walls, at last it entered the gloomy archway where it is supposed to have made its way to the vaults beneath and was no more seen. After a time the burrow was carefully filled up. To the satisfaction of the parishioners, there has been no return of the Ludham Dragon.

E

EGYPT

Many Norfolk churches have been transformed out of all recognition since they were originally constructed. The Reformation in the sixteenth century and the Puritan movement in the following century both resulted in great structural changes, with rood screens being taken down and religious icons destroyed. Before the widespread Victorian restoration movement, which led to sometimes drastic reconfiguring and fitting out, chancels had fallen out of use and were used as vestries, school rooms and even storage areas.

Not so at Saxlingham Church, though. Here, the chancel was filled with an enormous monument to Mirabel, the first wife of one of the lords of the manor, Sir Christopher Heydon. Although the memorial is no longer there, we have a wonderfully detailed description of it by the historian, Francis Blomefield. In his multivolume *An Essay Towards a Topographical History of the County of Norfolk*, published in the first half of the eighteenth century, Blomefield records that it was:

> A most curious and sumptuous monument, which takes up almost the whole area, inclosed with iron rails, there being just space enough left to go round the monument, which is raised in form of an Egyptian pyramid, of marble and stone, supported by pillars, and reaching almost to the top of the chancel, having an urn on the summit; in the arch under the pyramid, and which supports it, is the effigies of a lady kneeling on a cushion, with a desk before her, on which lies a Bible.

The pyramid was surrounded by life-size effigies of their eight children and was covered with many Egyptian hieroglyphs and astrological signs. Sir Christopher had travelled extensively overseas and so it was highly likely that he had seen the pyramids at Giza.

This rather bizarre monument was taken down in 1789, using the excuse, perhaps, that it had become a safety hazard. A visitor to Saxlingham Church today, though, can still see some remaining fragments in the form of the alabaster kneeling figure of Lady Mirabel, as well as her Bible.

★★★

The first, small intake of students to the new University of East Anglia (UEA) campus was in 1966 on a site on the outskirts of Norwich. The eminent English architect, Sir Denys Lasdun, had been chosen to design the university's core buildings. Lasdun's best-known design is the Royal National Theatre on London's South Bank. It is one of the most notable examples of Brutalist design in the country.

'The Ziggurats' of the University of East Anglia provide unique student accommodation. (Tony Scheuregger)

Brutalism emerged as an architectural style in the 1950s and is characterised by bare building materials such as concrete, steel, timber and glass. Denys Lasdun's vision for UEA was for a campus university with everything a student needed in close proximity. His design put all the teaching and research functions into a single 'teaching wall', which followed the contours of the site, alongside which he built a walkway giving access to the various buildings.

On the southern side of the walkway, he added groups of student residences. According to Lasdun, he designed these to recall 'vineyards in France ... or a rocky outcrop on a slope'. These Grade II listed terraced units, which became known as 'the Ziggurats', have attracted a great deal of interest over the years, as well as having won a number of awards.

Originating in ancient Mesopotamia, and therefore one of the oldest religious structures in the world, the ziggurat was a pyramidal, stepped tower that served as part of a temple complex. It is identifiable by stepped tiers that recede inward as the building rises. Unlike their near architectural cousins, the Egyptian pyramids, ziggurats were solid structures with no internal chambers. The sides and terraces were often landscaped with trees and shrubs, the most famous example being the Hanging Gardens of Babylon, one of the seven wonders of the ancient world.

***

The Blickling Estate extends to around 4,600 acres and dates back many centuries; it was mentioned in Domesday Book, compiled in 1086. Blickling is believed to have been the birthplace of Anne Boleyn, the ill-fated second wife of Henry VIII, but only the moat from the Boleyns' Tudor house remains.

The present red-brick hall was built by Sir Henry Hobart, who bought the estate in 1616. It was one of his female descendants who, in the early nineteenth century, transformed the gardens and parkland.

Caroline Hobart had inherited Blickling in 1793 on the death of her father. She and her husband, Lord Suffield, employed John Adey Repton, the son of famous landscape gardener Humphry Repton, to work with her at Blickling.

One of Blickling's most iconic landmarks is the mausoleum that Lady Caroline Suffield commissioned as a memorial and resting place for her father, Sir John Hobart, 2nd Earl of Buckinghamshire, whose death is said to have been self-inflicted but accidental – he plunged his gout-ridden foot into cold water.

The mausoleum sits on the edge of the estate's woodlands, near the lake, and is in the shape of a pyramid. It is built from 190,000 Portland stone bricks that would originally have gleamed white when the structure was completed. Here, Sir John and his two wives lie in marble tomb chests in the pyramid's burial chamber. Above the entrance to the mausoleum is the Hobart coat of arms and to the back is a sculpture of a bull – a nod to the family symbol of the Boleyn family.

Caroline engaged the architect Joseph Bonomi to design the memorial. He had spent the first twenty-eight years of his life in Rome and no doubt drew inspiration from the pyramid that was built as a tomb for Roman magistrate Caius Cestius, which still stands in the Italian capital. The Blickling pyramid is one third of the size of its Roman equivalent but is still a breathtaking sight, and certainly out of the ordinary in rural Norfolk.

★★★

Norfolk can, with some certainty, claim to have been the 'birthplace' of the most significant archaeological discovery in Egypt's Valley of the Kings – the tomb of the Pharoah, Tutankhamun. It was at Didlington Hall near Swaffham that the young Howard Carter first learned about ancient Egypt. Later in life, Carter wrote:

> It is to Lord and Lady Amherst that I owe an immense gratitude for their extreme kindness to me during my early career. It was the Amherst Egyptian collection, perhaps the largest and most interesting collection of its kind then in England, that aroused my longing for that county. It gave me an earnest desire to see Egypt.

Howard Carter spent much of his childhood in Swaffham, where both parents had been born, and it was his father, the artist and illustrator Samuel John Carter, who first took the 17-year-old Howard to Didlington Hall. It was then that Lady Amherst, who was so impressed by Howard Carter's drawings, suggested that he should go to Egypt to help record the tomb paintings then being unearthed. Within a few years, Howard's knowledge of ancient Egypt and skill at drawing and painting the discoveries saw him appointed Inspector of Monuments, based in Luxor. There, he led scientific and systematic excavations, which in turn led to him being hired by Lord Carnarvon to search for tombs that had been missed by previous expeditions, including that of the young pharaoh Tutankhamun.

William George Tyssen-Amherst had purchased Didlington Hall in 1853 and set about transforming the Georgian house into a sprawling Italianate mansion, which reportedly boasted eighty bedrooms. William's son, William Amherst Tyssen-Amherst, who inherited the estate in 1855, was an avid collector of books, manuscripts, antique furniture and other works of art. These included a 1456 copy of the Gutenberg Bible and another copy of the Bible that had been owned by Charles I.

Lord Amherst even built a museum wing at the house that housed his rapidly growing collection of Egyptian artefacts. These included ancient papyri and seven life-sized Sekhmet goddess figures, with human bodies and the heads of lionesses.

Tyssen-Amherst spent much time and energy, as well as money, on his Egyptian passion and this, sadly, led to the demise of his collection. He had entrusted the running of the house to his solicitor, who embezzled the assets to satisfy a gambling habit. Lord Amherst had no option but to sell, in 1909, his prized library of books in order to keep the estate running. He died shortly afterwards. In 1921, the collection of Egyptian antiquities was auctioned at Sotheby's. Howard Carter was closely involved in the sale and prepared the detailed catalogue himself.

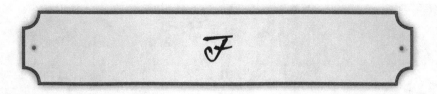

FIRE

Cow Tower is situated on a commanding position on a sharp bend on the banks of the River Wensum in Norwich. It stands some 15m high and 11m across with 1.8m-thick walls at the base of the round structure. These walls have a core of flint and are faced both inside and outside with bricks. Completed in 1399, the tower is considered to have some of the finest medieval brickwork in England.

The use of bricks for this sort of fortification was a shrewd, albeit expensive, choice as brick was known to absorb the impact of artillery fire better than stone. Cow Tower, which takes its name from the surrounding meadow previously known as Cowholme, was built to house guns and artillery men. It was specially designed to support the use of gunpowder artillery. Records show that by the late fourteenth century, Norwich had fifty gunpowder weapons, which it deployed at various locations along the city walls to defend it from invasion. The tower has several gunports around its circumference from which would be fired the smaller guns, as well as arrows, and the roof was capable of supporting larger cannon.

Cow Tower came under fire from Robert Kett and his army during the famous uprising in 1549. The riot had started because of hardships inflicted on the working classes by the extensive enclosure of common land. The rebels were intent on capturing the Bishop Bridge, which would have given them access into the city over the river. It stood a short distance from Cow Tower. Although the tower suffered some damage to its parapets, it proved impenetrable and the rebellion failed. Robert Kett was seized and taken to London with his brother William, where they were condemned to death for treason. Robert was brought back to Norwich and executed on 7 December 1549.

Cow Tower has played a key role in past centuries in defending Norfolk's capital from attack. (Tony Scheuregger)

***

Smuggling was one of the major crimes that occupied column space in eighteenth-century newspapers. This illegal trade along England's coast had grown at a prodigious rate. It became a large and lucrative industry despite the penalties imposed for those who were caught in the act.

This illicit dealing in perishable goods such as tea, coffee, gin and brandy came about as a direct result of the imposition of crippling taxation by successive governments, who were desperate to fund costly wars in Europe. It is hardly surprising, then, that Norfolk, with its long coastline, was a major centre for smuggling. When Daniel Defoe visited the region in the 1720s, he commented:

From Clye, we go to Masham, and to Wells, all towns on the coast, in each whereof there is a very considerable trade carried on with Holland for corn, which that part of the country is very full of: I say nothing of the great trade driven here from Holland, back again to England, because I take it to be trade carried on with much less honesty than advantage; especially while the clandestine trade or the art of smuggling was so much in practice.

The authorities waged a long and hard war against the smugglers. Excise officers on patrol were backed up by local, regular troops and yeomanry. If a band of smugglers was spotted, then often bloody fights ensued.

One notorious smuggling captain who worked along the Norfolk coast was William Kemble, who commanded the ship *Lively*, which brought contraband from Dunkirk. *The Norfolk Chronicle* tells of one fatal incident when Kemble's group of smugglers were confronted by government officials and soldiers in Old Hunstanton. Kemble and his men, in an attempt to regain their seized goods, opened fire with their guns. In the churchyard there, two gravestones tell of the ultimate outcome:

In memory of William Webb, late of the 15th Light Dragoons, who was shot from his horse by a party of smugglers on 25 September 1784 aged 26 years. I am not dead but sleepeth here, And when the Trumpet Sound I will appear. Four balls thro' me pearced there was. Hard it was I'd no time to pray. This stone that here you Do see My Comrades Erected for the sake of me.

Here lie the mangled remains of poor William Green, an Honest Officer of Government, who in the faithful discharge of his duty was inhumanly murdered by a gang of smugglers in this parish September 27, 1784, aged 37 years.

Three of the smugglers (including William Kemble) were captured, but despite the overwhelming evidence against them they were twice acquitted by juries at the Norfolk Assizes the following year.

★★★

On 22 September 1761, the citizens of Norwich were treated to a spectacular pyrotechnic display in the marketplace to celebrate the coronation of George III. A special triumphal arch had been constructed on which the fixed fireworks were mounted. Rockets were launched from the ground in front of the arch. Compared to the widely varied displays we are used to in the twenty-first century, the range of fireworks were relatively limited. The basic mixture of ingredients used in the eighteenth century did not make such intense colours; instead, the saltpetre, sulphur, charcoal, antimony and iron filings produced mainly sparks and the force necessary to propel the rockets into the air.

The eighteenth century witnessed a period of wealth for Norwich residents. The city's prosperity was due to the continued growth in its importance as a textile manufacturing centre.

Norwich society had a sizeable group of individuals who considered themselves the so-called 'middling sort'. They comprised tenant farmers, tradesmen and shopkeepers and they had both money and leisure time with which they wanted to enjoy themselves. Norwich, therefore, became one of the foremost entertainment venues in the country.

As well as balls, plays, concerts and operas, the residents of Georgian Norwich benefited from the springing up of pleasure gardens. It was one of a handful of cities in England where the rising 'middling sort' could enjoy these open spaces for walking and recreation. In 1739, John Moore designed New Spring Gardens as a place where ladies and gentlemen could promenade, take a pleasure boat ride or enjoy wines, cider, cakes and ale. Other Norwich pleasure gardens were Quantrell's, which lay just outside St Stephen's Gate, and Bunn's, on the other side of the city.

An illustration from the *Norwich Gazette* of fireworks at the coronation celebration of 1761.

Each appeared to compete with the other to put on the most enterprising entertainments. On 17 June 1788, for the admission price of 1s, spectators in the illuminated Quantrell's Gardens enjoyed a concert of vocal and instrumental music, followed by a firework display 'in the Italian taste', which included fountains of Chinese fire, balloon wheels with stars and serpents and a pyramid of Roman candles, as well as fixed stars and suns.

Such displays were not without risks, though. Bunn's Gardens suffered a tragedy in 1782 when fireworks were being prepared in an outhouse. The chemicals caught fire and exploded, killing one of the engineers outright. The fireworks were cancelled and a memorial concert held instead.

FLORA

In Long Gore Marsh on the Norfolk Broads, a curious pond is to be found. It covers three quarters of an acre and has turf islands in it in the form of a double-headed eagle holding Greek crosses and wearing a crown. Underneath this creature are the large initials 'MP'.

The pond was excavated to mark the 500th anniversary, in 1953, of the Fall of Byzantium to the Turks and was created by Marietta Pallis, an ecologist, painter and author. Born in 1882, Marietta was the daughter of a Greek scholar and poet. She studied natural sciences at Liverpool University, where she first surveyed the Norfolk Broads, resulting in a publication in 1909. In fact, in having her pool dug into the peaty marsh, Pallis was able to support the then new theory that the Broads developed because of medieval peat digging. It was dug by four men using traditional Norfolk marsh tools and when they reached of depth of around 3m, they discovered that the peat was impermeable to water.

Later, Marietta Pallis travelled and studied in the Danube delta, Greece and south-eastern Europe. After the First World War, Pallis spent her winters in London and her summers in a rented, marshland cottage at Long Gores, Hickling, a property she later bought. In the grounds she built a large thatched studio in which she reportedly recited the Greek Orthodox liturgy beneath a corona hung from the ceiling.

To add to the rather extraordinary nature of Pallis' pool, it is the last resting place of both the botanist herself, after her death in 1963, and her partner, Phyllis Clark, who had died in Cyprus in 1955 but had been reinterred at Long Gores in 1959. Their bodies are weighted down with large granite blocks to stop their coffins from floating to the surface of the water and their position is marked by two iron crosses in the central island.

★★★

The burial register for St Peter Mancroft, in the centre of Norwich, reveals many remarkable details about the lives and deaths of city folk over the centuries. However, perhaps one of the most curious and startling entries was made on 4 July 1922 when the incumbent buried just a skull of a man, reportedly 317 years old! This was no ordinary man, however, but the celebrated polymath – an individual of wide knowledge and learning – Sir Thomas Browne. The vicar gave the place of residence (!) as the Norfolk & Norwich Hospital Museum, where the skull had been since 1845. Some thirty years before this interment, the journal *Notes and Queries* reported on a current dispute over the remains of Browne:

> Considerable interest has been excited in Norwich by a dispute concerning the skull of Sir Thomas Browne, the writer of 'Religio Medici'. His body was interred in the chancel of St. Peter Mancroft Church, about a couple of centuries ago; and in 1840 some unknown person, in digging a vault, broke the lid of the coffin. His remains were examined by a local antiquary, who ordered the coffin and its contents to be re-interred. It appears, however, that the sexton took possession of the skull, which was purchased by a celebrated Norwich surgeon, and on his death was handed over to the Norfolk and Norwich Hospital Museum, where it now remains. Recently the attention of the Vicar of St. Peter Mancroft was called to the circumstances, and naturally regarding the removal as an act of desecration and dishonor, the Vestry requested the Hospital authorities to restore the skull of this illustrious man to its resting place. This application, however, has been refused; and at another vestry meeting it was agreed by eight votes to six, that no further steps should be taken.

The vicar was, however, rather determined and managed, finally, to retrieve the skull and rebury it.

Sir Thomas Browne studied and wrote on a diverse range of subjects including science and medicine, religion and the natural world. He had a particular interest in botany and zoology. He lived in Norwich for most of his adult life and had a house that stood where Hay Hill is now, next to the church in which he is buried, and where there is now a statue to probably one of Norwich's most famous residents.

Sir Thomas was a skilled physician who grew the ingredients of his medicines in his own garden. In addition to being a medical doctor, Browne was a keen naturalist and delighted in collecting curiosities, which included a live bittern and a stuffed dolphin. He was visited in his house by the famous diarist John Evelyn on 18 October 1671, who described what he saw:

> Next morning I went to see Sir Thomas Browne (with whom I had sometime corresponded by letters though never saw before) whose whole house & garden being a paradise and cabinet of rarities, & that of the best collection, especially medals, book, plants, natural things.

***

Nowadays, the small village of Hethel, 5 miles south-east of Wymondham, is best known as the home of Lotus Cars, which designs and builds high-end race and production cars. The company's headquarters is on the site of the former RAF Hethel, used by US bombers in the Second World War and then by RAF Fighter Command. Lotus uses the runways and taxiways as test tracks for its automobiles.

Within earshot of this hi-tech activity is the village churchyard where there stands the oldest known living hawthorn tree, certainly in East Anglia and probably in the UK. This single common hawthorn (*Crataegus monogyna*) forms the smallest reserve – covering just 0.025 hectares – looked after by the Norfolk Wildlife Trust and, in fact, of any wildlife trust in Britain.

Folk tales across the country tell of how a hawthorn bush grew from the staff of Joseph of Arimathea. This bush in Hethel dates back at least to the thirteenth century, when it was mentioned in deeds as a boundary marker, but local tradition has it that the hawthorn was a meeting place of rebels in the time of King John (which would make it more than 800 years old).

Hethel Old Thorn, drawn and engraved in the nineteenth century by Henry Ninham.

Although the Hethel Old Thorn is still healthy and continues to grow, it is considerably smaller than in previous centuries: in 1755, its girth was recorded as 9ft 1in and in 1841 the trunk was reportedly 12ft 1in circumference with the branches spread over 31 yards. Within living memory, villagers recall how children would dance around a Maypole and then scramble to the hawthorn to count the number of props holding up the branches.

GREEN

Norwich boasts a large expanse of green space, much of which is within a few miles of the city centre. In total, at last count, the local authority was responsible for twenty-three parks, ninety-five open spaces and fifty-nine natural areas. These include Bowthorpe Marsh, a 15-acre nature reserve adjacent to the River Yare; Lion Wood, recorded in the 1086 Domesday Book and home to many mature trees such as oak, sycamore, chestnut, beech, hornbeam and birch; and Mousehold Heath, the largest of the open spaces at 230 acres.

Norwich's parks are also many and varied, ranging from Chapelfield Gardens, opened in 1880, to Harford Park, with its cycle speedway track and a multiuse gaming area. Four further parks – Eaton, Heigham, Wensum and Waterloo – are Grade II listed and were purpose built in the 1920s and 1930s. The story of their creation is a fascinating tale of one man's vision and his determination to create spaces of recreation and relaxation for Norwich's residents.

In 1919, Captain Arnold Sandys-Winsch, a horticulturalist and landscape architect, was successful in his application to become the Parks Superintendent at Norwich City Council, a post he held until 1956. Like other British cities in the aftermath of the First World War, Norwich had a large number of unemployed people; the majority of these were men who had returned from military service and nearly 3,000 of these were registered for relief work.

Local schemes of work were needed to provide some level of employment to supplement the relatively low unemployment benefit payments. The city authorities therefore embarked on an ambitious programme of rebuilding and development, aided by funding secured from the government.

A large part of this activity was Captain Sandys-Winsch's plan for a series of formal parks, which would include structures and hard landscaping as well as wooded areas and flower beds. The captain designed large, open spaces with geometric designs and classical architecture.

The first to be completed, Heigham Park, opened in 1924 and included a small pond, sporting facilities and a children's playground. Wensum Park followed in the next year. A pavilion is one of the centrepieces of this riverside park.

The 80-acre Eaton Park, the flagship park, was opened by the Prince of Wales in 1928. Several of Sandys-Winsch's structures remain, including the central rotunda, a domed bandstand, the model boating pond and a lily pond. The park offers a wide range of sporting facilities as well as a miniature railway. Waterloo Park was opened in 1933 and boasts one of the largest herbaceous borders in any British public park.

By the late 1990s, many of the original modernist, pre-cast concrete structures in Captain Sandys-Winch's parks had fallen into disrepair. A successful application to the Heritage Lottery Fund has, however, enabled a programme of major refurbishment to all four of these parks and their architecture.

★★★

When most people conjure up in their minds an image of church fêtes, they think of tombola, cake stalls, bric-a-brac and perhaps the odd glass of home-made wine. While these undoubtedly feature at the annual summer fête at St Andrew's at Congham, near King's Lynn, there is one rather surprising – and, indeed, unique – offering. Every year for the past twenty-five years or so, Congham has played host to the World Snail Racing Championships. As one of the organisers puts it, 'Congham is to snail racing what Newmarket is to horse racing.'

The snails' racecourse is, of course, rather smaller than that at the famous Suffolk town. The small gastropods battle it out on a circular table covered with a wet white cloth with inner and outer circles drawn on it in red. The distance between the two is 13in. The snails, each with a numbered race sticker on the top of their shells, are put in the middle on the inner circle pointing outwards. The Snail Master then shouts, 'Ready, steady, SLOW!' to start the race and off go the snails. The current world record, which can only be set at these annual championships, was achieved back in the 1990s by a snail called Archie with a time of two minutes.

As with other world championships, the snail trainers take the competition extremely seriously and, apparently, children make better trainers than adults. Some even breed snails specially to compete in the races, concentrating on both diet and training to produce a champion. At the race itself, snails are paid close attention by their owners. As one trainer explained, 'Snails love the damp, so the trick is to sprinkle your snail with water before the race so it is wide awake.'

The annual event, however, is also open to novices: snails are available to hire on the day of the competition, which usually attracts a couple of hundred entrants who compete in heats with fifteen racers each. The grand final follows for the winners of each heat.

So, what does the champion get? Well, a silver tankard stuffed with lots of lovely green, fresh lettuce leaves!

★★★

There is a truly remarkable green space that remains almost entirely hidden from view from the public thoroughfare, and even though it is open 365 days a year, many Norwich residents are unaware of its existence! The Plantation Garden sits in a former chalk quarry in the shadow of the Catholic Cathedral of St John the Baptist and was created in the nineteenth century by a wealthy furniture maker, Henry Trevor. The garden covers less than

Even on a dull day, there are many delights to be found at Henry Trevor's Plantation Garden. (Tony Scheuregger)

3 acres, and yet, in this relatively small space, Trevor built himself a house at street level and a magical sunken garden that reflected his own rather eccentric and flamboyant tastes, combining Gothic and Italianate styles.

One of the surviving centrepieces of his garden, and indeed one of the first structures to be built, is the unique brick and flint fountain that bears the date 1857. Other features included a folly, a rustic bridge and a thatched summerhouse. By the 1870s, Henry had installed a large state-of-the-art, heated palm house, constructed by the Norwich firm Boulton & Paul. Other glasshouses also populated the garden, although all of those have long since disappeared.

Trevor always intended his fantasy garden to be enjoyed by family and friends, and they could do so by exploring the numerous walkways and promenades that snake their way up and down the terraced sides. All manner of brick and flint artefacts appear in the structure of the retaining walls and there is a wide variety of traditional flowerbed planting, woodlands and shrubberies.

Henry Trevor died in 1897 and successive tenants of Plantation House and Garden let the garden become severely neglected and overgrown. That is, until 1980, when the Plantation Garden Preservation Trust was formed and an army of dedicated volunteers began the long, painstaking work of transforming the wilderness to its former glory.

GREY

Of all the folktales handed down through generations of people living in the fenlands of Norfolk, one of the most remarkable is the story of how a humble feather saved a king.

It is said that, in times gone by, there was a secret society called the Brotherhood of the Grey Goose Feather. Any fenmen and fenwomen who found themselves in trouble, or indeed danger, need only to show a feather from a greylag goose with a split stem and they would be helped and protected by others without question.

During the English Civil War, Snore Hall near Downham Market was owned by Royalist Sir Ralph Skipwith, who risked his own life to shelter Charles I, who was on the run from Oliver Cromwell and his Roundhead troops. The monarch soon needed to move onwards to Huntingdon, where one of his men would be waiting to take him to safety in Oxford.

So, Charles I and his party of Cavaliers set out to cross the treacherous fens, aided by a local landlord who, to show his trustworthiness, had produced a split grey goose feather that he had handed to the king. This act was to prove a lifesaver for Charles, at least for a while. The River Ouse, which he needed to cross, was controlled by Cromwell's men but on being challenged by them, he showed the feather. Being locals themselves, the Roundhead soldiers allowed Charles and his entourage to pass.

Cromwell, who came from nearby Huntingdon, would also have been aware of the split goose feather tradition and on hearing that his own troops had let the monarch escape, said, 'It was better that the king escape than the old custom be broken.'

As we all know from our history books, sadly Charles I was not to escape Cromwell. The Roundheads later captured the king and he was sentenced to death. On the evening before the execution, legend has it that Cromwell was having supper when a messenger from the condemned king arrived, saying, 'The king is too proud to beg for mercy, but he asks you to give him the help that you would give anybody who carries this token', whereby the messenger dropped a split grey goose feather onto the table in front of Cromwell. He wrestled with his conscience all night but ultimately allowed the execution to proceed. It is said that Cromwell brooded on this decision for the rest of his life.

★★★

The county of Norfolk has its very own leaning tower, albeit not nearly as famous as the bell tower of Pisa Cathedral in Italy. It is believed that Greyfriars Tower in King's Lynn was only saved from the same fate that befell the rest of the medieval friary, of which the tower was the central part, because it could usefully serve as a marker for sailors and traders navigating the Wash. It now leans by 1 degree, compared with Pisa's 5.5 degrees. This modest tilt is, however, apparent to most observers.

Before Henry VIII dissolved the monasteries in England, there were sixty Franciscan friaries in the country; today, the significant remains of only sixteen exist. Franciscan friars, who followed St Francis of Assisi, adhered to vows of chastity, poverty and obedience and would have relied on the charity of townspeople for whom they performed pastoral duties. Franciscans were called Greyfriars after the colour of their religious habit, which was originally made from a greyish, unbleached wool.

Greyfriars Tower, taken from Thomas Kitson Cromwell's *Excursions Through Norfolk, Volume 2* (1819).

The Franciscan friary in King's Lynn was founded in the 1230s and a chronicle from this religious establishment dating from the fourteenth century survives, which describes how the Black Death arrived in this country from the Continent:

> In this year, 1348, in Melcombe in the county of Dorset, a little before the feast of St John the Baptist, two ships, one of them from Bristol came alongside. One of the sailors had brought them from Gascony the seeds of the terrible pestilence, and through him the men of that town of Melcombe were the first in England to be infected.

Today, the 'Leaning Tower of Lynn' sits in the attractive Tower Gardens, originally laid out in 1911 to mark the coronation of George V but which have been remodelled using hard landscaping to mark where other parts of the friary would once have been.

★★★

Over the centuries, the population of Norfolk has endured many outbreaks of plague. In 1578, Elizabeth I made a progress to East Anglia that culminated in a six-night stay in the Bishop's Palace next to the cathedral in Norwich.

It is thought that the queen was accompanied by an entourage of around 2,000 people, so perhaps it is not surprising that this large delegation from London brought the dreaded plague from the capital to East Anglia that summer. It is thought that at least 4,800 Norwich residents lost their lives in the wake of the royal visit due to this pestilence. Reports at the time described the illness:

> Such was its violence that all other distempers gave way to it or ran into it. They experienced a most intolerable pain from the heat of the head; the eyes were swelled and fiery; the tongue bloody; respiration difficult and breath fetid; vomitings of bilious matters frequent; finally the body became livid, with pimples here and there scattered over it, which bred worms. Death took place the second or third day.

Is this the Lady in Grey who haunts Tombland Alley? (Tony Scheuregger)

There is a disturbing tale that may or may not contain some elements of truth, but it is a story that nevertheless continues to intrigue residents and visitors alike. It is said that one Norwich family who succumbed to the plague in 1578 lived in the timber-framed house known as Augustine Steward's House, which sits on Tombland, directly opposite the Erpingham Gate. Such infected people would usually be moved out of their houses and then these properties would be locked up.

Sadly, often those who had already died of the plague were boarded up in their houses until the authorities had the opportunity to bury them. So, when this house was reopened some weeks later, officials discovered the bodies of two adults – the mother and father – together with the corpse of a young woman. On closer examination, the parents were found to have human teeth marks on their legs. They were even more horrified to find that the young woman had seemingly choked to death on pieces of human flesh they found in her windpipe – they had locked the daughter, who had still been alive, into the house with her dead parents. With no food or water to sustain her, the young woman had been forced to try to eat her parents' limbs.

Ever since these disturbing events, a young woman is said to haunt Tombland Alley, which runs alongside Augustine Steward's House. She is known as the Lady in Grey as she always appears in faded and ragged grey clothes. Occupants of the house have reported feeling the presence of the girl. Interestingly, and quite ironically, the property is currently used by a company offering escape room experiences.

H

HEADS

A casual visitor to Stow Bardolph Church is in for surprise, and even those who know what to expect are often unprepared for the encounter. In many respects, the mainly nineteenth-century church is much like any other. Even the presence of a family mausoleum, entered by a doorway on the north side of the chancel, is not unusual.

However, sharing this space with nineteen other memorials to the Hare family of Stow Hall, dating from the early 1600s, is a rather plain, unassuming wooden cabinet. A brass plaque on it reads:

> Here lyeth the body of Sarah Hare, youngest daughter of Sir Thomas Hare Bart and Dame Elizabeth his wife and sister to the present Sir Thomas Hare who departed this life the IX day of April MDCCXLIV and ordered this effigies [sic] to be placed here.

This, perhaps, is a clue as to what you might find within, and it is not for the faint-hearted. On opening the cabinet door, the visitor is confronted with a life-sized head, hands and torso in wax. I challenge anyone not to be shocked and spooked by this sight.

Although it is clearly a wax effigy and not Sarah Hare's actual corpse (which is buried in the mausoleum), it is not a pretty sight. Poor Sarah Hare was not a terribly beautiful woman, even accounting for the fact that she was 55 years old when she died. This wax mortuary statue is the only one of its kind outside of Westminster Abbey; most such statues at the time were made of marble.

Sarah Hare was the youngest daughter of Sir Thomas Hare. She remained unmarried and died in 1744, as a result of blood poisoning from having pricked her finger with a needle while sewing. It is said that she was in the habit of sewing on a Sunday, a practice that was frowned upon at the time and therefore she might have been said to have been struck down by will of God.

The previous year, Sarah had made a will that recorded:

> I desire to have my face and hands made in wax with a piece of crimson satin thrown like a garment in a picture hair upon my head and put in a case of mahogany with a glass before and fixed up so near the place where my corpse lies as it can be with my name and time of death put upon the case in any manner most desirable if I do not execute this in my life I desire it may be done after my death.

Her wishes were certainly adhered to rigidly, but we don't know whether the effigy was, in fact, created when she was alive or whether her executors had to attend to this rather eccentric matter after her death.

***

In November 1885, an appalling spectacle was witnessed by a handful of men at Norwich Castle Gaol. One of the invited local newspaper reporters was later to refer to the incident as 'the last judicial beheading in England', some 138 years after this form of capital punishment was supposedly last used. So, what happened at this curious Victorian execution?

The unfortunate criminal was Robert Goodale, a market gardener who lived and worked in Walsoken, a fenland village on the Norfolk–Cambridgeshire border. Goodale had been found guilty at the County Assizes in Norwich of the murder of his wife, Bathsheba, by battering her to death during an argument, after which he had thrown her lifeless body into a well.

Robert Goodale was sentenced to death by hanging and the services of the country's Chief Executioner, James Berry, were obtained to carry out the unenviable job of despatching the condemned man to the afterlife. Berry was highly respected and travelled the length and breadth of the country carrying out executions. However, before arriving in Norwich to execute Robert Goodale, the hangman had had a bad experience in Devon. Three unsuccessful attempts had been made to execute a prisoner, John Lee, where, despite the testing of the scaffold before each attempted hanging, the trapdoor failed to open. Lee was reprieved and his sentence commuted to life imprisonment.

Robert Goodale's hanging was scheduled for the morning of 30 November 1885 and James Berry had made all the necessary exacting preparations. He like to use 'tried and tested' ropes for execution and so brought along one he had used in Hereford the previous week. Berry had also carefully worked out the 'drop' of the prisoner using a prescribed table, giving the length of the drop against the weight of the condemned prisoner. Tests were also made to the gallows immediately prior to the execution.

At 8 a.m., Berry pulled the lever to open the trapdoor. As to what happened next, this is best left for James Berry to describe in his own words in a later memoir. He recorded:

> We were horrified to see the rope jerked upwards and for an instant I thought the noose had slipped from the culprit's head or that the rope had broken. It was worse than that for the jerk had severed the head entirely from the body and both had fallen into the bottom of the pit. Of course, death was instantaneous so that the poor fellow had not suffered in any way; but it was terrible to think such a revolting thing should have occurred. We were all unnerved and shocked.

A coroner's inquest into the manner of Robert Goodale's execution was deemed by the authorities to be necessary. Although James Berry was ultimately exonerated of any blame, this incident clearly haunted him. Berry retired in 1892 but not before he had contributed much to the science of hanging by the so-called long drop method, aimed at diminishing mental and physical suffering of the condemned.

A graphic artist's impression of the execution of the unfortunate Robert Goodale in the *Illustrated Police News*.

James Berry later converted to Christianity and became a prominent campaigner for the abolition of the death penalty. It was to be over half a century after Berry's death, though, before capital punishment for murder was finally abolished.

***

In 1609, a lawyer called Sir Edward Coke bought Neales Manor in the parish of Holkham, on the north Norfolk coast, and thus he founded what today we know as the Holkham Estate. It was one of Sir Edward's descendants, Thomas Coke, the 1st Earl of Leicester, who built the Palladian-style mansion between 1734 and 1764. Over the centuries, the Cokes of Holkham have been pioneers in farming, in particular.

In common with other large estates in the county, Holkham employed gamekeepers to manage the stock of birds and animals, which were subject to hunting and shooting for recreation, as well as for feeding the family and their guests. In the 1840s, a herd of fallow deer was introduced to Holkham. It was also in this decade that Edward Coke, younger brother of the 2nd Earl of Leicester, was instrumental in the creation of an iconic piece of headwear.

In the nineteenth century, gamekeepers traditionally wore top hats when on duty and Edward Coke recognised that these hats were ill-suited to their purpose, especially when the men encountered low-hanging branches or had to climb through undergrowth. On the other hand, the gamekeepers still needed some head protection, not least from any attacks from poachers. So, Edward approached a hatter in London to design a more sensible form of headwear.

Lock & Co., today the oldest hat shop in the world, tasked its chief hatmaker, Thomas Bowler, to produce a prototype. It is reported that when Edward Coke visited the company to inspect the hat, he placed it on the ground and jumped up and down on it to test its durability. It duly passed this test with flying colours and so the Coke hat, later to become known internationally as the bowler, was invented in 1849. Today, the 8th Earl of Leicester apparently continues to buy a Coke hat for his gamekeepers at Holkham to celebrate their completion of one year's service.

HEARTS

Broadsides were the tabloid newspapers of yesteryear before the widespread introduction of books and newspapers. They were printed on a single sheet of paper and often illustrated with a simple woodcut. They were therefore relatively easy and inexpensive to produce on early printing presses. Often, these broadsides were sold for just one penny, meaning that many people could afford to buy them and find out what was going on in the outside world.

Broadside ballads were the verses published in these papers, which were sometimes accompanied by the suggestion of a suitable popular tune to which the ballad could be sung. All sorts of topics were covered in these broadside ballads including political events, disasters, crime (including gruesome details of executions and other punishments), religion and love. One such ballad called 'The Unhappy Bride' was printed and sold by Lane & Walker of St Andrew's in Norwich and goes as follows:

Seven months I've been marry'd the more to my grief,
Seven months I've been marry'd, can find no relief,
Seven months I've been marry'd, and still I'm a maid,
I'm ruin'd, I'm ruin'd, I'm ruin'd, she said.

He brings me sugar-plumbs every night,
He calls me his jewel, and his heart's delight,
I'm his heart's delight, but an unhappy bride,
I'm ruin'd, I'm ruin'd, I'm ruin'd, she cry'd.

He brings me fine ribbons all flower'd with gold,
And many a fine story to me he has told,
But I do call on him like a bird in a tree,
I'm ruin'd, I'm ruin'd, I'm ruin'd, cry'd she.

My husband lies by me like one that's bewitch'd,
Not a hem of my garments he ever yet stitch'd,
But I do call on him like a poor distress'd wife,
I'm ruin'd, I'm ruin'd, all the days of my life.

I'd have you to do as your next neighbour's done,
To get me a delicate daughter or son,

For I long to enjoy that sweet gossiping crew,
I'm ruin'd, I'm ruin'd, and what shall I do.

My mother gives me ten acres of ground,
My father gives me five hundred pound,
I'll part with it all for the sake of a man,
I'm ruin'd, I'm ruin'd, do all that I can.

Sadly, we don't know whether this was a fictional account or the wailings of a real-life Norfolk wife. However, the tale of one young woman from Dereham did become a popular ballad.

In 1810, this lass lost her heart to a soldier who was serving in the 24th Regiment. Her sweetheart was sent off to war and unable to live without him, she resolved to follow him. She dressed in male clothing and headed to Norwich, where she enlisted in the army. However, she signed up to serve in the 54th Regiment by mistake and, soon after, her true gender was discovered, she was discharged and sent back to Dereham.

★★★

One unfortunate King's Lynn woman was the subject of a pamphlet written by a clergyman called Alexander Roberts. He was a demonologist who believed in the existence and powers of witches, as well as deserving punishments. Roberts' *A Treatise of Witchcraft* details the trial and execution in 1616 of Mary Smith, a cheesemaker. The Devil supposedly appeared to her in the form of a man who tempted her into renouncing God in exchange for gaining magical powers.

She cursed her first victim, who had reportedly hit her son, saying that she 'wished in a most earnest and bitter manner that his fingers might rotte off'. The poor man did indeed suffer this fate, nine months later, in both his fingers and toes. Another of Mary's victims, Elizabeth Hancock, was alleged to have stolen her hen and so she put a curse on Elizabeth so that she couldn't eat and wasted away. Having been tried and convicted, Mary Smith was hanged in the Tuesday Market Place in King's Lynn.

Another wretched woman to suffer the fate of having been accused of being a witch was Margaret Read, otherwise known as Shady Meg. In 1590, she had apparently cast a spell on the father of an illegitimate child. He was suddenly struck down with severe chest and stomach pains and died three

A 1613 'manual' on how to swim a suspected witch.

Witches Apprehended, Examined and Executed, for notable villanies by them committed both by Land and Water. With a strange and most true triall how to know whether a woman be a Witch or not.

Printed at London for *Edward Marchant*, and are to be sold at his shop ouer against the Crosse in Pauls Church-yard. 1 6 1 3.

days later. When the authorities searched Shady Meg's house, they found a small male figure with pins stuck into its chest and stomach.

This evidence sealed her fate, and she suffered the well-known method to prove whether someone was (or was not) a witch. It was thought that water rejected servants of the Devil. In 1653, Sir Robert Filmer described how the suspect would be stripped naked and then tied up with the right thumb to the left big toe and vice versa. In this position, they would be secured by ropes and thrown into a deep stream or pond three times. If they sank (and unfortunately often drowned), they were deemed innocent. However, if they floated they were guilty. Often men with long poles were employed to push them under the water while others, holding on to the ropes, pulled them up again.

Margaret Read floated and was one of just three women in England to be executed by burning. Tradition has it that during her execution at Tuesday Market Place, when her body was being consumed by the flames, Shady Meg's heart burst out of her body and hit the wall of one of the nearby houses, leaving a burn mark. If you look carefully above one of the windows, there is a carved, diamond pattern in black on the brickwork with a heart at its centre, marking the spot where Margaret Read's heart landed.

HORSES

There is a murky pond called Callow Pit on the boundary of Moulton St Mary and Cantley, which is said to be patrolled by a headless horseman at midnight. This mysterious ghost rides his steed between the pit and Cantley Spong, a mile away, and is said to guard a large iron chest full of gold, hidden deep in the pit's waters.

Legend also has it that the treasure chest was just visible through the dark water, the iron ring on the top of the box glinting in the sunlight. So, inevitably, there were those in the past who tried to raise and then plunder the sunken chest. *The East Anglian Handbook and Agricultural Annual for 1885*, itself an unexpected treasure trove of local folklore, recounts the story of two men who attempted to claim the gold:

They placed ladders horizontally across the water so as to form a bridge, and began groping with long poles in the depths beneath, at first unsuccessfully. Persevering, however, they at length struck some hard substance, and feeling cautiously around it with their staves, they found a large ring on its upper surface, through which, after some trouble, they managed to pass a stout pole, and with great exertion raised a huge iron-bound box to the surface, and on to their platform. Overcome with glee at their haul, one of the men couldn't contain his joy and cried out: 'Ha! We've got it now! Even Old Nick shan't take it from us!' The words had scarcely left his lips when suddenly, the pair were enveloped in a thick cloud of sulphurous vapour – they watched in horror as, from the choking mist, a black hand and arm rose through the water and grasped the chest. They struggled manfully for their mysterious booty [...] but the infernal grip was too much for the box, which sank with a splash into the pit, leaving the ring still upon the pole. Crest-fallen, the disappointed treasure-seekers wended their way home without the prize for which they had toiled so hard, and in memory of their adventure caused the ring to be affixed as a handle on the door of Southwood Church.

The so-called Devil's Doorknocker on the church's door was removed when the church fell into disrepair in the 1880s and was instead placed on the north door of the nearby church of St Botolph in Limpenhoe. This is an apt siting given that, traditionally, the north door of a church is sometimes referred to as the Devil's Door after a belief in the Middle Ages that the Devil lived in an unbaptised child's soul. At the baby's christening, the Devil would be driven out of the child and had to be able to leave. Accordingly, a door was often built into the north wall for this purpose.

★★★

Hunstanton beach in 1934, ruled over
by the Lord High Admiral of the Wash.
(George Plunkett)

The Le Strange family have had their
ancestral home in Old Hunstanton
since they came over from France
after William the Conqueror defeated
Harold at the Battle of Hastings. In
the fifteenth and sixteenth centuries,
the Le Stranges were one of the most
powerful Norfolk families, during
which time they built Hunstanton
Hall, a large moated house surrounded
by parkland, woodland and gardens.

One of the more unusual honours to have been bestowed is that of Lord
High Admiral of the Wash, an ancient hereditary office granted to the Le
Strange family. With the title came the responsibility for the defence and
protection of the entire coastal area of the Wash. Along with these duties,
came the rights to this part of the Norfolk coast for as far as a man on
horseback could ride out to sea at low tide and throw a javelin! When the
Royal Navy took over the defence of the area in the sixteenth century,
the post of Lord High Admiral became obsolete, but it was never formally
abolished and has continued to be handed down through the generations.

On 29 June 1929, a long-since almost forgotten British endurance
swimmer named Mercedes Gleitze completed a marathon swim of 25 miles
in thirteen hours and seventeen minutes across the Wash. In doing so, she
became the first person ever to have completed this feat. A journalist who
recorded Gleitze's swim wrote:

> The conditions at the outset were ideal, but as the day wore on a strong
> wind sprang up and the sea became very choppy. Tremendous difficulties
> with the tide were experienced and so strong was the current in the latter
> stages of the swim that Miss Gleitze battled bravely against it for four hours
> without making any appreciable headway.

Nevertheless, the swimmer did complete the challenge and was reportedly greeted by several hundred people, who gave her a rousing reception and carried her out of the water. Apparently, one of those standing on the shore was the Lord High Admiral of the Wash, who greeted Mercedes with the words, 'You do understand, madam, that everything washed up on this beach belongs to me?'

***

The village of Walsingham, a few miles from the north Norfolk coastline, boasts a wealth of historic buildings dating back to the eleventh century. It is a place where pilgrims have flocked to for over 900 years, since a Saxon noblewoman, Richeldis de Faverches, is said to have had a vision where she was taken by Mary, the mother of Jesus, to her home in Nazareth. In this vision, Richeldis was asked by Mary to build an exact copy of this house in Walsingham, which she did.

By the Middle Ages, the shrine to Our Lady, situated in the Augustinian priory at Walsingham, was arguably the most important place of pilgrimage in England. Today, only a small fraction of the original abbey building remains, including the spectacular east end arch, and the grounds attract many tourists each year to the 18 acres of stunning grounds and gardens.

One of a number of listed Historic England structures on the priory's estate is a packhorse bridge straddling the River Stiffkey, although it is not as old as it seems. It is very probably a late seventeenth or early eighteenth-century interpretation of an earlier medieval bridge that may have crossed the river at another point nearby. It incorporates stones from the medieval priory, including some highly decorative ones featuring faces. It is the only one of its kind that survives in Norfolk, although other counties have more than one.

Such river crossings were intended to carry horses loaded with saddle bags and panniers and were typically built with one or more narrow masonry arches and low parapets (so that the horse with its panniers on either side would not get stuck). The bridges sprung up on major trading routes across the country.

Interestingly, one of the other listed buildings in Walsingham is the public toilets in the High Street, adjacent to the abbey's gatehouse. They are the only Grade I listed public conveniences in the country!

INK

Norwich has a long and successful tradition of printing, dating back to the time of Elizabeth I. However, the first book to be published in the city was printed in Dutch by one of the so-called 'Strangers'. In the mid-sixteenth century, the dominant textile industry in Norwich suddenly suffered an economic downturn due to the success of lighter, foreign fabrics arriving on the scene to rival Norfolk's worsted cloth. The city's mayor, Thomas Sotherton, and other dignitaries came up with an idea to invite master weavers from the Low Countries to settle in Norwich. So, in 1566, the first thirty Strangers, many of these Protestant refugees, arrived followed by many more in the next decade or so. By 1579, there were 6,000 Strangers in the city out of a population of about 16,000.

In the late summer or autumn of 1567, Anthony de Solempne (or Solemne) arrived in Norwich with his wife and two sons. From surviving records, he appears to have been one of the wealthiest members of the Stranger community, having been a spice merchant in his native Brabant in the southern Netherlands. Solempne became a well-respected member of the Dutch congregation in Norwich and later served as one of its elders. He also swapped his spice dealing in favour of two professions: a vendor of wine from the German Rhineland and a printer.

He established his business at the sign of the White Dove in the parish of St John, Maddermarket. In fact, Solempne established the first-known printing press in the city, and barely a year after his arrival published the first book printed in Norwich. This religious publication was in his native Dutch language and the title can be translated as *Confession of Faith*. A copy of it survives in the Norfolk Library and Information Service.

Dove Street was the birthplace of the printing trade in Norwich. (Tony Scheuregger)

Most of Solempne's books are in his native language, like *An Historical Perpetual Calendar*, which came out in 1570 and 'in which you will find the rising and setting of the Sun in every month, with the fairs in divers counties, towns and liberties'. However, the Dutchman also published some books and pamphlets in English and French, including a 1572 broadsheet entitled *A Prayer to be Sayd in the End of the Mornyng Prayer Daily (through the Dioeces of Norwich) during the Tyme of this Sharp Wether, of Frost and Snow*.

★★★

The eighteenth century witnessed the introduction of regional newspapers in the country. In fact, *The Norwich Post* was England's first provincial paper and was published by Francis Burges on 6 September 1701.

The content of this weekly newspaper, though, was far from local. Although the numerous advertisements in the early issues are for all manner of goods, services and property in the county, the newspaper contained 'An account of the most remarkable transactions both foreign and domestick'.

Other prominent early rags followed, including the *Norwich Mercury*, *Norfolk Chronicle* and the *Norfolk News*. The editors of these publications soon realised that the more sensational and local their content, the more likely they were to sell copies. They covered reports of crimes dealt with in the Petty Sessions, the forerunners of the Magistrates' Courts, and the more serious crimes such as fraud and murder tried at the regular Assizes, presided over by a visiting judge. These trials were often recorded verbatim in the newspapers.

On 28 November 1848, one of the most shocking crimes of the nineteenth century was committed that, although tragic for the victims and their families, provided fodder for journalistic reporting in Norfolk's newspapers for many months. The double murder of Isaac Jermy and his son, Isaac, at Stanfield Hall hit both the national and local headlines when the two men were shot and killed on the porch and in the hallway of their mansion near Wymondham.

Police soon apprehended a suspect, James Bloomfield Rush, who was the Jermys' tenant farmer. He had, it appeared, carried out a complex and devious scheme to defraud the Jermys of their property, which involved getting rid of them, their family and servant.

Mrs Jermy and the servant, who both survived the attack despite being badly wounded, would later identify the badly disguised Rush as the killer. Evidence from these witnesses was vivid and dramatic and was lapped up by readers of the various newspapers.

On 31 March 1849, the *Norfolk News* even published an 'Extraordinary' supplement to its usual edition that devoted several pages to Rush's trial at the County Assizes. To allow its readers to follow the report more easily, it was accompanied by an illustration of Stanfield Hall, as well as floorplans of the house and a map of the surrounding area.

The farmer was found guilty and sentenced to death. Those Norwich residents who were unable to attend the public hanging on 21 April were, of course, able to read a blow-by-blow account in the *Norfolk News*, of which this is an abbreviated version(!):

The short distance between the Castle entrance and the drop was lined on one side by the magistrates of the county and on the other by representatives of the press. At last the death-knell began to toll from the spire of St. Peter's Mancroft, and shortly after twelve o'clock the dreadful procession emerged from the Castle, and took its way to the drop … The wretched prisoner moved along with great firmness. He was dressed in black, wore patent leather boots, and had his shirt collar, which was scrupulously clean, turned over. As his head was bare, the features of his face could be distinctly marked … His step never faltered, and he regularly marched to his doom. On catching sight of the scaffold, he lifted his eyes to heaven, raised as far as he could his pinioned hands, and shook his head mournfully from side to side once or twice. The pantomime was perfect, conveying almost as clearly as words a protest of innocence, combined with resignation of his fate … The wretched man then mounted the scaffold, but instead of looking to the crowd, he turned his face to the Castle walls, the white night-cap was placed over his head, and fastening the fatal rope to the beam, adjusted the noose to his neck. The unhappy man, even at this dreadful moment, had not lost his coolness. 'This does not go easy,' he said, 'put the thing a little higher, take your time, don't be in a hurry'. These were his last words. The rope was in the right place, the drop fell, and in an instant the murderer was dead. No struggles ensued, and the dreadful ceremony was performed as quickly and as well as is practicable and with fewer revolting circumstances than usual. During the whole time the crowd without maintained a solemn silence, and the only sounds that accompanied the fall of the body, and jerking of the tightened rope were one or two faint shrieks. After being suspended for one hour, it was cut down and carried back to the Castle where interment took place within the precincts.

***

In Norwich, in 1752, a man was born who, through his success in his chosen profession, would lead to the creation of two words in the English language. He was the son of a manufacturer in the city and was sent to

Norwich-born Luke Hansard, who lent his name to two words in the English dictionary.

a grammar school in his mother's home county of Lincolnshire, where he received a traditional, classical education.

After serving an apprenticeship to Stephen White, a printer in Cockey Lane in Norwich, Luke's term as an apprentice ended with his father's death and so he moved to London. Here, he found work as a compositor in the firm of John Hughes, Printer to the House of Commons.

Luke Hansard worked his way up the ranks to become a partner, before taking over the firm in 1800. When two of his sons joined him in business, the firm became Luke Hansard & Sons. One of these, Thomas Curson Hansard, was responsible in 1809 for publishing William Cobbett's *Parliamentary Debates* and, three years later, after Cobbett had stood trial for seditious libel, the family firm took over proprietorship of this publication, which was renamed *Hansard Parliamentary Debates* and has been abbreviated over time to *Hansard*. This has become an accepted proper noun in English dictionaries. In addition, in April 1868, the Earl of Derby created the verb 'hansardise', which is defined by *Chambers English Dictionary* as 'to confront someone with his former recorded opinion'.

In the 1880s, Her Majesty's Stationery Office (HMSO) took over as the publisher of the official record of proceedings in both Houses of Parliament from Hansard and in 1909, Parliament became responsible for publishing the transcripts of all its debates. By coincidence, when HMSO relocated out of London, it came to Norwich, where Sovereign House, a bold symbol of 1960s architecture, became its headquarters. This now-abandoned building stands across the road from the Church of St Mary's, Coslany, where Luke Hansard was christened.

★★★

Charles Dickens is regarded by many as the greatest novelist of the Victorian era. It is his keen observations of society and topical events, reflected in all his books and short stories, which mark him out as a literary genius. His novels are as readable today as they were during his lifetime.

Of course, Dickens needed people and places to provide inspiration for his writing, and from his pen flowed many memorable characters, often based on actual people. One Norfolk man immortalised by Charles Dickens was James Sharman. Sharman had been a sailor aboard HMS *Victory* at the Battle of Trafalgar and had helped carry Lord Nelson below deck after he was fatally wounded. He lived in Great Yarmouth, where he became the first keeper of the Nelson Monument in the town.

A few decades after the famous sea battle, Sharman performed an act of great bravery in rescuing the crew of a ship that was wrecked on the beach near his cottage. It is said that on reading a newspaper report of the rescue, Dickens was moved to visit Sharman in Yarmouth and then based his character Ham Peggotty in *David Copperfield* on him. In the novel, there is a description of Ham, who drowns trying to rescue James Steerforth during a storm at sea, which reads:

> He was a huge, strong fellow of six feet high, broad in proportion, and round-shouldered; but with a simpering boy's face and curly light hair that gave him quite a sheepish look. He was dressed in a canvas jacket, and a pair of such very stiff trousers that they would have stood quite as well alone, without any legs in them. And you couldn't so properly have said he wore a hat, as that he was covered in a-top, like an old building, with something pitchy.

I wonder how accurate a picture of James Sharman this is.

Charles Dickens reportedly loved Norfolk, although in 1849, in a private letter to his literary agent, he refers to Great Yarmouth, the location for *David Copperfield*, as 'a spongy and soppy place'! In *The Pickwick Papers*, Mr Pickwick and Sam Weller have some memorable adventures in Norfolk and a description in the book of an election at Eatanswill is believed to be a light-hearted comment on Norwich residents. Dickens writes, 'The Eatanswill people, like the people of many other small towns, considered themselves of the utmost and most mighty importance.'

JEWS

It is perhaps a little-known fact that at the time of the Norman invasion of England in 1066, Norfolk was already the richest and most populous part of the country. Along with the Normans came other people from abroad and in Norwich an early French community was established, as well as a Jewish quarter. These foreign incomers represented around 4 per cent of the population of the city.

The first recorded Jewish person in Norwich was in 1086 and it is probable that Jews were encouraged to settle in the shadow of the castle so that they could be protected from anti-Semitism. The Normans needed the Jews in Norwich to act primarily as money lenders: at this time, it was a sin for Christians to make a profit from money lending and so the Jewish community provided the necessary loans for the city to grow economically. This Jewish quarter, or Jewry, had a synagogue in its centre, its own cemetery nearby and a separate Jewish school, which was situated in the south of the quarter. As an indication of how important and active they were, a third of all surviving Hebrew and half of the Latin deeds drawn up in this country concerning Anglo-Jewish transactions originate from Norwich's Jews.

The wealthiest Jew in the twelfth century in Norwich, and indeed in the country, was Isaac Jurnet. Although it was thought that Isaac had the large stone house in King Street constructed, it is now believed that it was his son – also called Isaac – who bought the property in 1225. The house we see today is mainly seventeenth century, although a twelfth-century vaulted undercroft (which would have been at street level when first built) still survives. The building has been through many transformations in its long existence and is now known as Wensum Lodge.

During the reign of Elizabeth I, the house became the headquarters of the Norwich waits (musicians) and was then known as the Music House. In Tudor times, any self-respecting town and city in the country would have its own band of waits. Their main duties were to play music for official and civic occasions, often in processions or as part of pageants and plays.

★★★

In March 1144, a 12-year-old boy was cruelly murdered on Mousehold Heath, overlooking Norwich. It led, eventually, to the persecution of the Jews in Norfolk, but not before the cult of St William had sprung up.

The mutilated body of a young skinner's apprentice called William was found by locals after reportedly being enticed away by the Jewish community, who had befriended him. There was no evidence as to the perpetrators of this heinous crime, but the boy's family pointed the finger at the Jews. It was claimed that they had crucified him after their synagogue service, using William's blood to make matzah (unleavened bread) for Passover.

However, the sheriff protected them and gave them refuge in the castle precincts, so no legal proceedings were brought against the Jewish community. William's body was moved to the cathedral, where it was claimed it had the 'odour of sanctity' and it was this fact, and other miracles concerning William's body, that led to calls for William to be canonised. He never was, although he was locally known as St William of Norwich.

The crucifixion of William as depicted on a rood screen in Holy Trinity Church, Loddon.

After William was buried, legend tells that a rose tree blossomed on his tomb until nearly Christmas. A woman who was having a difficult labour drank water that had had a fern from William's grave steeped in it. She safely gave birth to a son. A man who was 'vexed by an unclean spirit' was tied up all night next to William's grave and, in the morning, he was cured. Other miracles included a lame boy being able to walk again after visiting the burial site.

William's uncle was accused of profiting from the boy's death by selling medicine supposedly made from water in which the gag found in William's mouth had been dipped. Remarkably, the cult of St William continued until the middle of the fourteenth century.

★★★

In 2004, when the foundations were being prepared for the Chapelfield Shopping Centre (currently called Chantry Place), the remains of seventeen bodies – adults and children – were found at the bottom of a medieval well. They appeared to have been thrown down the well at the same time, all head first, with the children having been thrown in after the adults. The skeletons have been since dated to the twelfth century and from recent DNA analysis we know that they were Ashkenazi Jews.

Experts' findings also revealed that four of the people had been related, including three sisters, the youngest having been 5 and the oldest a young adult. No evidence of disease was found by the scientists examining the skeletons and the location of the bodies – thrown into the well rather than buried – suggested that they had probably been murdered and their bodies callously disposed of, out of sight.

The most compelling theory as to the circumstances surrounding these deaths is that these people were victims of an anti-Semitic massacre in 1190. In his *Ymagines Historiarum*, dating from the early years of the thirteenth century, the chronicler Ralph de Diceto recorded, 'Accordingly on 6th February all the Jews who were found in their own houses at Norwich were butchered; some had taken refuge in the castle'.

On 19 March 2013, all seventeen bodies were finally laid to rest at a ceremony in the Jewish part of Earlham Cemetery.

KINGS

Norfolk did not bring King John a great deal of luck. The monarch had acceded to the throne of England in 1199 but his reign was dogged by challenges to the Crown from inside his kingdom, as well as further afield.

He was not a popular ruler. In 1215, rebel barons had forced him to assent to Magna Carta, a charter of liberty and political rights, but John tried to resist its implementation and therefore continued to be threatened by the rebels, who had a stronghold in East Anglia.

In September 1216, the king launched a campaign to retake these counties, taking his crown jewels with him for safekeeping and reaching King's Lynn to gather supplies. However, he was also fleeing Prince Louis of France, who had landed unopposed in Kent earlier in the year, as well as the Scottish King Alexander II, who had already headed south having invaded the north of England.

King John, already weakened by illness, decided to head north from King's Lynn to confront Alexander. This involved crossing the Wash. The body of water is a tidal estuary, which contains quicksand and tidal whirlpools.

What happened next is, of course, not terribly well documented but it appears that John lost part of his baggage train in the Wash, along with several horses. Most importantly, he is said to have lost his crown jewels. These were never recovered and they have been eagerly sought by treasure hunters ever since.

A fourteenth-century depiction of King John hunting a stag with his hounds.

★★★

Great Yarmouth has, for many centuries, been famed for its herring fishery. In the eleventh century, William the Conqueror gave lands valued at 3 shillings a year to be added to the Manor of Carlton on condition that the lord of the manor should provide the royal court with twenty-four herring pies or pasties each year, each pie being made from 100 herrings. When Yarmouth took possession of the manor, they were obliged to continue this practice.

One of the further stipulations was that the pies should be made using the first herrings of the season. Another was that they should be taken to wherever the king was in the country at that time. For his troubles, the bearer of the pies received six white loaves, one flagon of wine, one flagon of beer, one truss of hay, one pricket of wax and six tallow candles.

This practice appears to have run smoothly under successive monarchs until 1629, when a letter from the household of Charles I was received by the mayor and sheriffs of Great Yarmouth, complaining about both the making and delivery of that year's pies. It read:

> Firstly, you do not send them according to your tenure, or the first new herrings that are taken. Secondly, you do not cause them to be well baked in good and strong pastye, as they ought to be that they may endure the carriage better. Thirdly, whereas you should by your tenure bake in these pasties six score herrings, at the least, being the great hundreth which does require five to be put into the pye at least, we find but fewer herrings to be in divers of them. Fourthly, the number of pies that you sent at this time, we finde to be fewer than have been sent heretofore, and diverse of them also much broken. And lastly, we understand the bringer of them was constrained to make three several journeys to you before he could have them whereas it seemeth he is bound to come but once.

It seems, though, that the matter was somehow rectified as the Great Yarmouth authorities continued to supply herring pies to the monarch until about 1829, when they were finally released from their obligation. Presumably royal tastes had altered!

★★★

Although Anglia Television was not one of the first Independent Television Authority stations to go on air, the name has proved one of the most enduring for several generations of viewers. It launched in 1959 to serve the East of England, using as its studios the former Agricultural Hall in Norwich. The company produced nationally known programmes such as *Sale of the Century*, *Tales of the Unexpected* and *Survival*, its flagship nature documentary series that ran to over 900 episodes. Today, it operates as ITV Anglia, broadcasting primarily news from a state-of-the-art facility in Norwich.

The iconic Anglia Television knight was used as the company's logo from 1959 through to 1988. Each appearance of the rotating knight was accompanied by a passage from Handel's *Water Music* arranged by the conductor and composer, Sir Malcolm Sargent.

The knight started life as a trophy that was commissioned by King William III of the Netherlands in 1850 for the Falcon Club, a society that met once a year to compete in horse races, falconry and other sports. The 22kg sterling-silver figure is modelled on the statue of Richard I that stands outside the Palace of Westminster, but it was intended to represent the Black Prince, the eldest son of Edward III.

It is said that Anglia Television's chairman, Lord Townshend spotted the trophy in a Bond Street jeweller's shop and bought it on an impulse to use as the ident for the soon-to-launch station. He had the statue altered to include the Anglia pennant on the lance held by the knight.

★★★

The English Reformation and the subsequent Dissolution of the Monasteries changed the face of Norfolk forever. When Henry VIII broke away from the Catholic Church and declared himself head of the Church of England, he started on a course that was to see the power shift from the Church to the State.

The reasons why the king decided to suppress the various religious orders are many and complex, but it is clear that he saw these Catholic institutions as centres of opposition to his break from Rome and the Pope. On Dissolution, vast amounts of monastic land, gold and silver plate were transferred to the Crown. The gentry who acquired great swathes of the land previously owned by these religious institutions also prospered.

At the time of the Dissolution in 1535, the priory at Old Buckenham was run by the aged Prior Millgate, who sent a letter to Henry's chief minister Thomas Cromwell, enclosing a fee and writing:

> … beseeching that we may obtain your favourable licence for the keeping of one cure and one chapel with four masses in the week day […] and may also put some of the laymen of their house in trust for employing their pasture and receiving their rents.

When the suppression commissioners finally got to Old Buckenham, they reported:

> This priory of black canons was of the clear annual value of 143 pounds, 7 shillings and 8 pence [...] The bells and lead £180 [...] stocks and stores, 117 pounds, 9 shillings and 7 pence [...] and the woodland around was worth 233 pounds, 6 shillings and 8 pence.

Sir Edmund Knyvett of Buckenham Castle was fast to act here, obtaining a lease of the priory site and its lands.

The Priory of Our Lady at Thetford was one of the largest, as well as one of the most important monasteries in medieval East Anglia. It had been founded at the beginning of the twelfth century and for 400 years it was the burial place of the Earls and Dukes of Norfolk. In 1536, the priory was threatened with suppression and the 3rd Duke of Norfolk petitioned Henry VIII to convert it into a college of secular canons. He pointed out that he was preparing in the church not only his own tomb, but also one for the king's own illegitimate son, Henry Fitzroy, Duke of Richmond. The Duke of Norfolk's petition failed and in February 1540, the last prior and sixteen monks were surrendered to Henry VIII's commissioners.

Wymondham Abbey's last abbot, Elisha Ferrers, became Vicar of Wymondham, enjoying a handsome pension. (Tony Scheuregger)

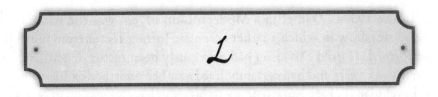

LIONS

In the fourteenth century, East Anglia, and in particular, Norwich, was an important centre for religious manuscript production. Abbeys and monasteries, as well as private individuals, commissioned elaborate illustrated manuscripts of religious texts. Many surviving examples were clearly aimed at the luxury end of the market and demonstrate the exceptional craftsmanship, imagination and artistry of these scribes.

The Macclesfield Psalter (named after its former owner, the Earl of Macclesfield) is now held at the Fitzwilliam Museum in Cambridge and is thought to have been made in the 1330s in Norfolk and it is probably the most remarkable English illuminated manuscript still in existence. This tiny book containing the 150 Old Testament psalms demonstrates that our medieval forebears had a keen sense of humour. The illustrations, with their bright colours and gilding still shining, include men with faces on their bottoms and legs growing from their shoulders. Many feature animals depicted undertaking human activities, such as a rabbit riding a hound and a dog dressed as a bishop. Although many of the creatures are those that would have been found in England at the time, other more exotic and imaginary creatures appear in the pages, including an ape mixing up medicinal remedies for a bear and a half-man, half-lion.

★★★

Another Old Testament book is Daniel, which tells of how the prophet Daniel was thrown into a lion's den because he would not renounce his faith in God. God sends an angel to shut the mouths of the beasts and Daniel is brought out unharmed.

In the 1930s, 'Daniel in a Modern Lion's Den' was the name of a circus sideshow in which a rather eccentric former rector from Norfolk performed. Harold Davidson had previously been rector of Stiffkey for twenty-six years and had certainly lived a rather unorthodox lifestyle for a churchman. In between attending to his church congregation in Norfolk at weekends, Davidson was accustomed to spending much of the week in London, engaged in various kinds of social work. He also became chaplain to the Actors' Church Union and was frequently to be found backstage in London theatres.

Harold Davidson also travelled to Paris, acting as chaperone for dancers at the famous cabaret music hall, the Folies Bergère. Visitors to the Stiffkey rectory, where his long-suffering wife remained, included many would-be actresses.

After serving in the Royal Navy as a chaplain during the First World War, Davidson returned to Stiffkey, and also resumed his London work, often dealing with fallen women. He saw it as his mission to try to find employment, as well as safe board and lodging, for these girls. He even styled himself as the 'Prostitutes' Padre'.

As you might imagine, there were those – especially in his Stiffkey parish – who were not happy with how their rector was choosing to spend his time. Accusations of Davidson associating with 'women of loose character' and 'accosting, molesting, and importuning young females for immoral purposes' followed, which culminated in Davidson being defrocked by the church authorities. Davidson protested his innocence for the rest of his life, much of which was spent performing in the amusement parks in fashionable seaside resorts such as Blackpool.

It was in Skegness that Davidson met his death. His act consisted of a ten-minute address to the fee-paying audience outside a cage containing two lions, after which he would enter the cage for a couple of minutes. On the evening of 28 July 1937, however, according to the former rector's biographer, Ronald Blythe, 'in scarcely credible terms, the little clergyman from Norfolk and the lion acted out the classical Christian martyrdom to the full'. One of the lions had become agitated and knocked Davidson unconscious. He died in hospital two days later, but not before reportedly uttering his last words, 'Did I make the front page?'

M

MAD

A man known across the country as 'Mad Windham' certainly started to earn this reputation at an early age. At the age of 4, William Frederick Windham, born in 1840 in Erpingham, was diagnosed by the chief surgeon at the Norwich Bethel Hospital as having 'degenerative weakness of mind'.

William was expelled from one of his prep schools for using foul language and was later removed from Eton. He was, by all accounts, a teenage tearaway, preferring 'low company and low pursuits' and was described as looking and behaving 'like a wild animal' and eating 'more like a brute than a rational being'. It was during his schooldays that his fellow pupils nicknamed him 'Mad Windham'; an epithet that stayed with him until his death at the age of just 25.

In August 1861, Windham inherited Felbrigg Hall in north Norfolk from his father and soon after, he married a woman of whom his uncle General Windham, did not approve – the same uncle who Windham decided to prevent from inheriting his estate by signing a deed to that effect. The ensuing legal case, brought by General Windham in an effort to prove that William

THE
GREAT LUNACY CASE
OF
MR. W. F. WINDHAM.
REPORTED BY A SOLICITOR.

Mr. WINDHAM, AS HE APPEARED IN COURT.

PRICE TWOPENCE.

LONDON: H. VICKERS, HOLYWELL STREET.

The public were able to read all the juicy details of the Windham lunacy case for just twopence.

was a lunatic and therefore incapable of making his own decisions, caused a public sensation. It was the longest and most expensive lunacy case in English history.

The general public were on William Windham's side and even the press opined that the case threatened to set a dangerous precedent and a threat to liberty if William was declared a lunatic just because he led an unorthodox life. William won the case but went on to fritter away his fortune, declaring himself bankrupt and selling Felbrigg Hall in 1863. In addition to a published pamphlet that described the court case in detail, William became the subject of a ballad that told his story. The chorus of this ballad went:

> It is a shame, and what's their game,
> To a madhouse try to send him,
> Money, money that's the thing,
> But they won't get over Windham.

★★★

A century earlier than Mad Windham, there was, in this county, arguably an equally mad aristocrat called George Walpole. George inherited the title of Earl of Orford and the large Norfolk estate of Houghton Hall, in 1751 at the age of 20, from his father, Robert. George's parents had separated shortly after his birth and so his father had moved his mistress, a celebrated singer and actress, into Houghton Hall.

George's mother was described as 'a woman of very singular character and considered half mad'. So, perhaps, George was destined to become increasingly eccentric throughout his life, eventually dying, insane, at 61 years of age. He was succeeded by his uncle, Horace, who once described George as 'the most ruined young man in England' and 'his whole pleasure is outrageous exercise'.

George Walpole was certainly mad about all kinds of sports including horseracing, hunting, bull baiting, fishing, cockfighting, as well as coursing and hawking. The earl helped found the Falconers' Society and for the 1783 hawking season he had fifty-two peregrines, goshawks and gyrfalcons. He also established the Swaffham Coursing Club. His kennels held fifty brace of greyhounds, including every sort of crossbreed he could try. George even tried to breed a bulldog cross and reportedly, after seven generations of breeding, got the best greyhounds of the time. They had 'small ears, rat tails and skins almost without hair, together with that innate courage rather to die than relinquish the chase'.

There were also rather more bizarre sporting exploits such as the December 1756 match against Lord Rockingham to race five turkeys against five Norfolk geese along the roads from Norwich to London's Mile End. The winner was to receive £500 from his opponent and so the stakes were high and the birds were trained strenuously. It is believed that George Walpole won the race with his geese because when nightfall came, Rockingham's turkeys went up into the trees to roost whereas Walpole was able to continue to drive his geese overnight.

MINUTES

In 2017, the Norwich Society, whose Civic Environment Committee carries out an annual survey, decided to focus on public clocks and sundials. They confined themselves to those within the boundary of the city of Norwich but, even so, the committee members were astonished to find over sixty timepieces. They varied greatly in shape, design and size and I must confess that since reading their report, I can't stop looking around for them!

There is a long history of clockmaking in Norwich, with the first clockmakers arriving from overseas in the first half of the seventeenth century. The van Barton family were one of these and Ahasuerus Fromanteel, a native of Norwich but of Flemish descent, was the first maker of pendulum clocks, which proved far more accurate than their predecessors.

In fact, Norwich has continued to lead the competition in the clockmaking profession. In the 1970s, Barclays Bank commissioned Martin Burgess to make the Gurney Clock for a site in Chapelfield Gardens. The bank wanted to commemorate the bicentenary of its presence in the city, having been founded as Gurney's Bank in 1775 on what was then Bank Plain. The design of the clock incorporated a lion and castle, representing the city of Norwich, and a pair of scales, representing the bank, and was a copy of a design by John Harrison (1693–1776), who famously won a reward of £20,000 in 1775 for inventing a chronometer accurate enough for navigators to determine their longitude at sea to half a degree.

Sadly, by the 1990s, the Gurney Clock had been vandalised in its original location and was soon to reappear in the Castle Mall shopping centre. The clock was removed from the centre in 2015 when renovations were carried out on the shops and has yet to see the light of day again.

★★★

The current large clock above the entrance to the south transept of Norwich Cathedral has completely different external and internal faces. It has a manual mechanism that required winding once a week by the vergers.

Although this version only dates from 1830, the priory's Sacrist's Rolls from 1322 to 1325 record the construction and installation, in the same place in the cathedral, of a large astronomical clock with automata – the earliest of its kind recorded in England. It featured a painted and gilt moon, a sun of gilt copper and brass pointers on the dial. It cost £52 9s 6d to build, equivalent to several tens of thousands of pounds in modern currency, and was expensive to maintain. This medieval clock was destroyed by fire in the sixteenth century and was replaced by a simpler one.

★★★

The time gun atop Norwich Castle was taken down in 1938. (George Plunkett)

From August 1900 to May 1938, Norwich Castle's battlements sported a curious time gun, which fired at 10 a.m. each day and allowed residents to check their own timepieces for accuracy once a day. It was triggered electronically from Greenwich using an electromagnet and detonator. At first, an iron ball was used but it was soon found to be damaging the fabric of the keep and so a lighter ball of wood and canvas was later substituted. The time gun was declared redundant and dismantled when time signals broadcast over the radio were introduced.

★★★

It was the rather shrewd Bishop of Thetford, Herbert de Losinga, who, in 1101, first thought to build the Church of St Margaret on a site between the rivers Purfleet and Mill Fleet where they discharged into the Wash. Thus, he founded the medieval town of Bishop's Lynn, which was granted a charter to hold a market on a Saturday next to the church.

Trade soon built up along the waterways and the town quickly expanded, adding another large marketplace to the north which held a weekly market on a Tuesday. By the fourteenth century, Bishop's Lynn ranked as England's most important port and was part of the Hanseatic League of ports, which dominated sea trade across Europe. After the Dissolution of the Monasteries by Henry VIII, Lynn changed its name to King's Lynn when it was ceded to the Crown while remaining a thriving and active port.

St Margaret's Church is now known as King's Lynn Minster and has one particularly unusual clock on the south tower at the building's western end. Part of the clock dates from around 1690 but most is a faithful, twentieth-century reproduction of this original.

It does not tell the time, instead it indicates when the tide in the port is at its height. In place of the usual numbers around the outside of the dial are letters which read 'LYNN HIGH TIDE' and are arranged on the even hours, two hours apart, making a twenty-four-hour clock. The pointer is, of course, also out of the ordinary, being a depiction of a green dragon sticking out his tongue. His tongue shows the time of the next high tide on the River Great Ouse. The clock also shows the phases of the moon using a blue disc which revolves with the dragon and a mechanism that controls an image of the moon, which revolves behind a hole in the disc.

★★★

Despite having found curious people, happenings and places at almost every turn in Norfolk, I am surprised that the county does not seem to have as many true follies as other counties. A folly is essentially a building constructed primarily for decoration, but suggesting through its appearance some other purpose, often grander than the reality. This criterion certainly applies to the Palladian-style Waterhouse on the Houghton Hall Estate, constructed in 1731 for Sir Robert Walpole. Arguably, though, it was never meant to be seen as anything other than a water tower, albeit a rather posh, stylish one!

One true Norfolk folly overlooks the River Wensum at Thorpe St Andrew, on the outskirts of Norwich. It is a turreted brick and flint tower and is thought to have been constructed in the 1800s. It echoes the design of Pinebanks, the house in whose grounds the tower stands.

Above the west doorway of the tower is an inscription from the Roman lyric poet, Horace, reading, '*Omne tulit punctum qui miscuit utile dulci*', which translates as, 'He has gained every point who has combined the useful and the agreeable'.

Another inscription, on a shield, tells us that 'HM Queen Kapiolani ascended this tower 6 June 1887'. The Queen of the Kingdom of Hawaii toured England on the occasion of the Golden Jubilee of Queen Victoria and, for reasons now shrouded in the mysteries of time, visited Norwich.

The villagers of Little Ellingham near Attleborough are so proud of their folly that it features prominently on their village sign alongside the village church, even although the folly itself stands not too distant from the sign. It was built in 1855 and is an over-large clock tower constructed in the grounds of Little Ellingham Hall.

The brick tower is built in three stages with a cupola on the top. The clock is only on the east side, with the other three faces of the square tower featuring blank roundels. At the foot of the tower on each of the four sides are two-storey cottages, forming a crucifix footprint. The village's clock tower is deemed important enough to be designated as a Grade II listed building: the hall itself does not merit this!

★★★

In 1602, a visitor to the Church of All Saint's in West Acre, near Swaffham, described the building as 'wholly decaied and ruynated' and thirty or so years later, the lord of the manor, Sir Edward Barkham almost completely rebuilt the church, reusing many pieces of dressed stone from the nearby priory. Since then, the villagers have clearly poured a lot of love, money and time into maintaining and enhancing the building, both inside and out. The chancel features some rather interesting carved wooden panels in both the reredos and altar front. It is believed that these came from a four-poster bed which belonged to a former vicar and the candle holders either side of the altar are said to have been the posts of the bed!

The other particularly striking feature of West Acre church is the clock on the tower, which dates from about 1910. It was paid for by the lord of the manor's daughter, Susan Birkbeck, in memory of her sister, Frances.

The clock was made by J. Smith & Sons of Derby and its face is unusual in that it features letters instead of numbers. The letters read, 'WATCH AND PRAY', and this phrase is taken from the Gospel of St Matthew where Christ says to his disciples in the Garden of Gethsemane, 'Watch and pray, that ye enter not into temptation: the spirit indeed is willing, but the flesh is weak'.

Such a dial on a church is rare, there probably only being four others in the country. The copper dial of West Acre's clock is painted black and the lettering is 23½-carat gold leaf. Inevitably, the dial is adversely affected by the weather and requires regular renovation. Experts who have previously worked on the clock face have noticed several dents in the copper dial and it is thought that someone has, in the past, aimed an air rifle at it.

n

NOTES

There are no fewer than four separate memorials in Norwich to one woman whose invention led to a system now used the world over. It was later refined by another individual, many say without her permission, but did she, in fact, invent this method? Well, the answer is, frankly, no, although she was responsible for transforming an ancient technique into a system fit for purpose in the modern era.

Sarah Glover was born in The Close in Norwich in 1786, the daughter of a clergyman. Like other girls of her social class, she and her sisters received a good, basic education that would have included learning social skills such as dancing and music. Sarah received music lessons from the organist of Norwich Cathedral at the relatively young age of 6, and so it is very possible that a particular musical talent was spotted by her parents.

In 1811, Reverend Glover became curate at St Laurence's Church in Norwich, and Sarah and her sister, Christiana, led the music-making at the services. They were also responsible for teaching the Sunday School and it was while attempting to teach her young charges to sing the hymn tunes, that Sarah developed a method to help these children learn the melodies.

Her system was a relatively straightforward one in that the first note of a scale was always called DOH, the second RAY, the third ME and so on. Her choir's excellent singing, due to Sarah Glover's teaching methods, soon gained such a reputation that young women from all over the country were being sent to Norwich to be trained by Sarah.

Alongside their church responsibilities, the Glover sisters opened a school for girls in Black Boy Yard, off Colegate, where Sarah perfected her so-called 'Norwich Sol-fa' system. It is, though, interesting to note how similar Sarah's invention is to one devised by Guido of Arezzo, an Italian music theorist and teacher who was active in the early eleventh century. His notation system is said to have used the initial syllables of each of the

Left: Sarah Glover holding her 'invention'; Right: Was Guido of Arezzo the true inventor of the Tonic Sol-fa system?

major philosophical concepts of the Middle Ages, to create *ut*(or *do*)-*re-mi-fa-sol-la-si* to represent the notes of a musical scale.

In the 1840s, Sarah Glover's 'new' Norwich Sol-fa method was further developed and enlarged by Reverend John Curwen into the Tonic Sol-fa system, which is still in widespread use today to teach sight singing. It is said that he very belatedly acknowledged that Sarah Glover's earlier invention had informed his own thinking.

So, when you next sit and watch the Von Trapp family in *The Sound of Music*, please spare a thought for Sarah Glover of Norwich who first popularised such a simple system of learning to sing.

***

The 30m tower of St Helen's Church in Ranworth – known as the Cathedral of the Broads – looms over the Bure Valley. The fifteenth-century church is remarkable in that it contains no fewer than three treasures of international importance. One of these is housed in a bulletproof secure case made by inmates of Norwich Prison and is known as the Ranworth Antiphoner.

It is a large singing book, dating from around 1460, and contains the words and music for psalms, hymns and responses which were read or sung alternately (antiphonally) by the priest and the choir. Its 285 vellum pages are illustrated with brightly coloured and gilded images, including nineteen lavishly illuminated capital letters. One depicts King David playing his harp and another shows several priests or monks, as well as a boy, standing round a cantor's desk singing from an antiphoner, perhaps the manuscript it actually appears in!

The book was probably commissioned of local scribes by a private individual or family and may be the antiphoner left to the church by William Cobb in his will of 1478. The antiphoner was used in the church before the Reformation, then it disappeared for 300 years, probably having been kept safe from destruction by a Catholic family. Ranworth's treasure was then rediscovered in the collection of a merchant banker, when it was bought in 1911, and returned to St Helen's. Before the Reformation, every parish church in the country would have owned and used at least one antiphoner: today, only Ranworth does so.

***

In the days of silent movies, when there was no soundtrack, cinemas would employ pianists to improvise music to fit with the mood of the film. In due course, the pianists were replaced by the more spectacular cinema organist and specially constructed organs began to appear – literally, because often they were installed in the cinemas so that they would mechanically rise to floor level for the film showings!

Undoubtedly, the king of cinema organs was the flamboyant Wurlitzer. However, the age of the mighty cinema organ was short-lived after the advent of talking pictures which could be accompanied by a musical soundtrack.

So, what happened to the Wurlitzers? Well, two of the grandest ever to have made their way to England, ended up in a Norfolk farmyard and in a car showroom in Diss.

In the 1970s, I remember as a child looking forward to car trips with my father to Kitchen Brothers' garage in Victoria Road in Diss. We were not, however, looking to purchase the latest Ford. Sitting, seemingly quite comfortably, next

Reverend Michael Booker at the console of the mighty Wurlitzer organ in Diss.
(Private collection)

to the gleaming new cars was a three-manual (keyboard) Wurlitzer cinema
organ – the third largest in the country – upon which my father would spend
many a happy hour playing all the show and seaside entertainment favourites
to the delight of motor dealers, Revel and Derek Kitchen.

The instrument had been rescued from the Paramount Cinema in
Newcastle and installed in the Diss showroom which had been specifically
built to house the organ console and its 1,350 pipes. Sadly, the Wurlitzer
only stayed ten years before it was dismantled once again in 1982 and
moved to a new entertainment complex in Northampton.

Another similar Wurlitzer travelled from Leeds to Norfolk in 1976 to be
installed in one of farmer George Cushing's barns. It took pride of place
alongside his growing collection of steam traction engines and fairground
organs. The Thursford Collection now attracts over 100,000 visitors
every year, who not only visit the museum but also flock to the famous
Christmas Spectacular, a three-hour-long live entertainment by over 100
musicians, singers and dancers, who perform alongside the organs and
merry-go-rounds.

***

You must delve quite deeply to make the connection between Northrepps and the unusual musical instrument on its village sign. This stringed instrument is a cittern which, by the seventeenth century, would have been found hanging on the wall of barbers' shops so that customers waiting to have their hair cut or their beard trimmed would have something to strum to while away the time.

It had a distinctive sound due to its metal strings, as opposed to other stringed instruments of the Renaissance era which had gut strings. It was John Playford who popularised the cittern as an instrument to accompany, among other things, dancing in the 1600s.

John was born in Norwich in 1623 and became a music publisher based in London. By far his most well-known publication is *The English Dancing Master*, a highly successful manual, which was produced in several editions by Playford and his successors. It contains the music and instructions on the relevant steps for over 100 English country dances. John Playford also wrote *Musick's Delight on the Cithren* in 1666, which contained arrangements for the cittern of many of these dances.

The parish Church of St Mary the Virgin in Northrepps largely dates from the fifteenth century and one feature from this time is the rood screen that separates the main body of the church from the chancel, where the priests and choir sat. The wooden screen has not, however, been there for all this time. In fact, it was only moved back to the church in 1911 after it was discovered in a local barn. Nobody really knows where it had been and when, but much of the carving is Victorian.

There is a very faint dedication written on it, much of which is illegible. This is thought to be genuinely medieval and the name that can be made out is John Playford. If this is the original donor of the screen, then this was a man who lived two centuries before John Playford, the publisher. Is there a connection, therefore? Well, perhaps an ancestral connection has been made between the well-known Northrepps Playfords and John, or perhaps it was a leap of faith on the part of the villagers who, nevertheless, have produced a colourful and interesting village sign.

OVERSEAS

Norfolk residents have been emigrating to America for over 400 years and the county can rightly lay claim to having spawned some of the prominent people in US history. A woman called Temperance Flowerdew left her home in Hethersett in 1609 and sailed on the *Falcon*, one of a convoy of nine ships bound for the New World. She came from a well-connected family, being the great-niece of Amy Robsart, the first wife of Robert Dudley, Earl of Leicester and favourite of Elizabeth I.

Temperance was one of the few survivors of the so-called 'starving time', during the winter of 1609–10 which killed almost 90 per cent of the population of Jamestown. There, she eventually met and married Sir George Yeardley, who was to become the Governor of Virginia, with Temperance becoming the First Lady of America. On Yeardley's death, Temperance became one of the wealthiest women in Virginia.

Another early pilgrim to America was Samuel Lincoln of Hingham. He sailed from Great Yarmouth in 1638, arriving in Salem, Massachusetts, and started the now famous American Lincoln dynasty.

The family moved from Hingham to Pennsylvania, Virginia and Kentucky. It was here, in 1809, that Abraham Lincoln, the future 16th President of the United States, was born. It is due to these early settlers that numerous placenames, like Hingham, in the United States are named after Norfolk towns and villages. In Massachusetts alone, we find Attleboro, Raynham, Walpole and Yarmouth. There are also no fewer than five Windhams (using the more accessible phonetic spelling of Wymondham!) and six places called Norwich.

★★★

Probably one of the most famous Native American women of all time not only had links with Norfolk but came to live in the county after her marriage to John Rolfe. The younger generation are now familiar with her story, albeit slightly romanticised, through the Walt Disney animated musical film which bears her name. It tells of how Pocahontas reportedly saved the life of the Englishman John Smith, who had settled in Jamestown, Virginia. Later, she married the tobacco planter John Rolfe.

John's wife and daughter had died on the voyage to Virginia and he agonised over marrying a heathen, even though Pocahontas had already converted to Christianity and adopted the baptismal name Rebecca. He was clearly infatuated with her, as he wrote to Thomas Dale, the Governor of Virginia, saying:

> … motivated not by the unbridled desire of carnal affection, but for the good of this plantation, for the honor of our country, for the Glory of God, for my own salvation […] namely Pocahontas, to whom my hearty and best thoughts are, and have been a long time so entangled, and enthralled in so intricate a labyrinth that I was even a-wearied to unwind myself thereout.

In 1616, John Rolfe returned to England with his new wife, where they lived in Middlesex and at Rolfe's family home at Heacham.

A pilgrim family flees persecution in England.

***

In a letter to *The Spectator* magazine in March 1972, Sir Thomas Hildebrand Preston, 6th Baronet Preston of Beeston Hall, Beeston St Lawrence, wrote, 'I have been haunted by the idea that had I been able to argue with the Ural Soviet for a longer period I might have been able to save the Russian Royal family'.

Thomas Preston had succeeded to the baronetcy late in life – at the age of 77 – on the death of his cousin, having spent a career in the Diplomatic Service, most of this overseas. Preston had joined the Foreign Office in about 1910, after having gone on gold-mining expeditions in northern Siberia, and three years later, he was appointed British Vice Consul in Ekaterinburg in Russia. It was there that, in April 1918, Tsar Nicholas II and his family were brought to spend what turned out to be the last two months of their lives before being murdered by the Bolsheviks.

As Preston wrote to *The Spectator*, 'From the window of my Consulate, I saw the Tsar being driven in a car from the station to the House Epatiev, which was the scene of the assassination.' Thomas Preston was later accused of having tried to rescue the royal family and was sentenced to death. He only escaped execution because of the timely capture of Ekaterinburg by friendly forces.

Sir Thomas Preston brought several mementos of his time in Russia back to England which, in due course, were installed in Beeston Hall. These included a painting of a regiment of Russian soldiers who had acted as the Russian royal family's escort, a candelabra, fire screen and samovar, a decorated metal tea urn.

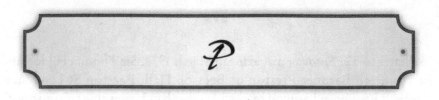

PERIL

We now take it for granted that when lives are in danger at sea, lifeboat crews based around the coast are ready and waiting to answer the call for action, putting their own lives at risk as they do so. The bravery of such heroes as Henry Blogg, Coxswain of the Cromer lifeboat for thirty-eight years, is still rightly celebrated.

In 1805, Cromer had been the second seaside town in Norfolk to get a purpose-built lifeboat. During Blogg's total of fifty-three years' service in the Royal National Lifeboat Institution (RNLI), the lifeboat was launched 287 times and saved 873 lives. Blogg was to become the most decorated lifeboatman in the history of the RNLI and his awards included the George Cross, which he was awarded in 1941. He also received the RNLI gold medal (the lifeboatman's Victoria Cross) three times and three silver medals, as well as the British Empire Medal.

★★★

Captain George William Manby was another Norfolk man who contributed to saving lives at sea. Rather than being a seaman, he was an army officer, but in 1807, when serving as barrack master at Great Yarmouth, he witnessed the wrecking of the naval ship HMS *Snipe* following a storm. Around 200 people, including French prisoners of war, were drowned, despite being just 60 yards from the shore.

This experience inspired him to revisit an experiment that Manby had conducted as a youth, when he had shot a mortar carrying a line over Downham Market Church, near his family home of Wood Hall, Hilgay. After further experiments, Captain Manby invented the Manby Mortar, which allowed a light rope attached to a rocket to be fired from the shore to a distressed ship. After being secured on the ship, the rope was then used to pull aboard from the shore a heavier rope that was strong enough to winch people on board the stricken ship to safety.

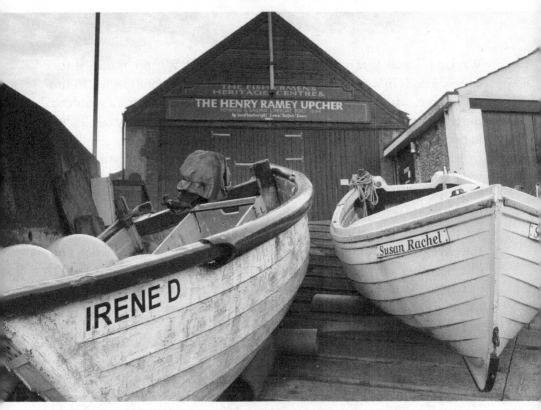

The old Sheringham lifeboat house. (Tony Scheuregger)

Captain Manby was well aware of the success of his invention and erected at his Yarmouth home a slate plaque on which he had inscribed the following:

In commemoration of the 12th of February 1808 on which day directly eastward of this spot the first life was saved from shipwreck, by means of a rope attached to a shot propelled by the force of gunpowder over the stranded vessel a method now universally adopted and to which at least 1000 sailors from different nations owe their preservation 1842.

Manby is buried in the churchyard at All Saints, Hilgay, and a nearby plaque reads, 'In the churchyard near this spot rest the bones of George William Manby, Captain. F.R.S. A name to be remembered as long as there is a stranded ship.'

***

Wayland Wood, just outside the market town of Watton, is one of the largest woods in south Norfolk and boasts over 125 plant species. In the springtime, with its stunning carpet of bluebells, it is hard for a visitor to the woodland to believe that it is the alleged setting of the fairy tale 'Babes in the Wood'.

It is a children's story about two children who, after the death of their wealthy parents, are left in the care of their uncle and aunt who live on the edge of a wood. If the children were to die before reaching maturity and inheriting their father's fortune, the money would go directly to the uncle. So, this wicked uncle takes the children into the wood and leaves them at the mercy of two would-be murderers. These two scoundrels fall out, one kills the other and then abandons the youngsters.

Lost in the woodlands, the children die and are covered with leaves by the robins. Their uncle, however, is guilt-ridden then imprisoned for debt and dies.

One of several woodcuts dating from 1700 that illustrated the published story of the 'Babes in the Wood'.

The tale was first published in 1595 as an anonymous broadside ballad by Thomas Millington in Norwich, under the title *The Norfolk gent his will and Testament and howe he Commytted the keepinge of his Children to his own brother whoe delte most wickedly with them and howe God plagued him for it.*

Folklore has it that the events took place in Wayland Wood and that the wicked uncle lived at the nearby Griston Hall. When, in 1879, the tree under which the babes had reputedly been abandoned was struck by lightning and destroyed, the popularity of the legend had grown to such an extent that people visited the site, hoping for souvenirs. The ghosts of the children are said to haunt the woods and a local nickname for the woodland – Wailing Wood – is due to the cries of the frightened and hungry children that can still be heard to this day.

PIGS

The ruins of St Benet's Abbey, on the banks of the River Bure in the Norfolk Broads, presents a rather sad if not ominous face to the world on even the brightest of summer days. In winter, it exudes a brooding and sorrowful atmosphere and in the autumn mists, the abbey is just downright spooky. It is not surprising, then, that there is not one, but two ghost stories attached to St Benedict's-at-Holm Abbey, to give the monastic institution its full name.

There is the story of Brother Pacifus, a skilled artist who had lent his expertise to repairing the rood screen at nearby Ranworth Church. Every morning at dawn, Pacifus would row the 2 miles along the river to Ranworth and then return the same way in the evening. One day, however, on returning to the abbey, he found it silent, emptied of its fellow monks. The abbey had been sacked by Henry VIII's men and the monks slaughtered.

The broken-hearted survivor became a hermit in the ruins and is still said to appear, rowing a boat, with his dog sitting in it, along that stretch of the Broads. Sadly, even those who believe in ghosts will soon realise that the tale has little basis in truth. In fact, St Benet's was the only monastic institution in the whole country not to have been officially closed by Henry VIII. The holder of the position of Bishop of Norwich is also, therefore, the Abbot of St Benet's and once a year, on 1 August, the bishop arrives along the river in the bow of a traditional wherry and preaches at a service.

The remains of the later windmill dwarf the ruins of the former gatehouse of St Benet's Abbey. (Tony Scheuregger)

Perhaps it is just as well that the Bishop of Norwich's annual visit is in August, because another ghost is said to appear every 25 May when a dark deed is said to have taken place. Ethelwold was a young monk who lived at St Benet's in Norman times, when the abbey was one of the last outposts of Saxon resistance against King William.

According to legend, Ethelwold was persuaded to ensure that the doors of the abbey were left unbolted so that the king's soldiers, who had laid siege to it, could gain entry. Instead of being paid handsomely for this treacherous deed, Ethelwold asked the Norman army to make him the abbot for life.

The Normans entered the abbey the following night and were herded into the church, where the invaders duly invested Ethelwold as the new abbot. They then dragged him to the bell tower, put a noose around his neck and hanged him. The Normans had kept their word. Ethelwold had been made abbot for life but, to this day, on the anniversary of his death, the screams, 'like a stuck pig', of the traitor monk are said to shatter the silence of the surrounding area.

★★★

The village of Heydon, near the market town of Reepham, is still one of Norfolk's best-kept secrets. The manor house, Heydon Hall, the estate and, in fact, the whole of the village are now in the hands of the Bulwer Long family.

Heydon is one of only a dozen or so English villages that are entirely privately owned. It retains the old-fashioned character of a small community huddled around a village green, partly because no new buildings have been added in the whole of the parish since the Jubilee Memorial Well House was built on the village green in 1887. Even then, this structure is an example of Tudor Revival architecture.

In recent years, the number of businesses has increased, following careful restoration of barns and other outbuildings. However, the population remains at around 100 people, all of whom are tenants of the manor.

With its hotchpotch of historic buildings in such an idyllic setting, and its lack of through traffic, it is no wonder that Heydon makes an ideal film location. In the early days of Anglia Television, it hosted the soap opera *Weavers Green*, as well as a sitcom about the Women's Land Army in the Second World War called *Backs to the Land*. It also featured in a Monty Python's Flying Circus sketch about village idiots, where they can be seen fooling around outside one of the houses and then sitting on the wall of a terraced row of cottages. They also appear outside the former school.

The tearooms at Heydon once played host to *The Peppermint Pig*. (Tony Scheuregger)

Films shot partly in the village or at the hall include *A Cock and Bull Story*, based on the novel *Tristram Shandy* by Laurence Sterne, *The Grotesque*, starring Sting, and *The Moonstone*. The television miniseries, *Love on a Branch Line* also used Heydon as a set, as did the television adaptation of Nina Bawden's novel *The Peppermint Pig*.

Heydon is perhaps best known for providing several of the locations in the 1970 film starring Julie Christie, *The Go-Between*. In the novel by L.P. Hartley, the elderly Leo Colston discovers a diary from the year 1900 in which is recorded the events of a summer he spent as a guest of the Maudsley family at the fictional Brandham Hall in Norfolk. Heydon Church was used when the Maudsley family went to worship and one of the houses on the village green was used repeatedly as a background shot and for the final interior scene where Leo and Marian discuss the past, which, as the opening line in the novel says, 'is a foreign country; they do things differently there'.

PUNCH

Reffley Spring Wood is a semi-ancient woodland now to be found at the centre of a residential housing estate in King's Lynn. Here is the site of a unique small red-brick temple once guarded by two stone sphinxes, which was built in 1789 but with its origins dating back to the previous century.

During the English Civil War, King's Lynn was a Royalist stronghold but, to save St Margaret's Church from bombardment by Oliver Cromwell's troops, the town surrendered to the Roundheads. Cromwell issued an order wthat forbade the assembly of more than thirty men, presumably aimed at neutralising any major opposition, and this is when the Sons of Reffley are said to have come into existence as an underground movement in support of the king. Its membership was limited to thirty and this has continued ever since.

After the Restoration of the monarchy in 1660, the Reffley Brethren, as they were also known, adopted the simple aims of the club, which were conviviality and good fellowship. Other than that, they had no fixed policy, no political affiliation or charitable objects. They met annually to spend an evening smoking the society's special mixture in their long clay pipes and drinking a freshly made punch.

This punch was brewed from a secret recipe known only to the secretary of the Sons and the brewer, who was one of the members. The principal ingredient was water from the natural spring that bubbled nearby. Above the spring an obelisk was erected dedicated to 'Bacchus and Venus, the gods of this place'. The last public meeting of the Sons of Reffley was in 1978 and four years later the temple, which had been vandalised, was demolished. It is understood that the society still meets, although not at Reffley Spring.

★★★

It was a Norfolk butcher who was the champion of what is thought to have been the first international heavyweight boxing match in 1750. John 'Jack' Slack, a bare-knuckle boxer, was reputedly the grandson of the first ever bare-knuckle fighter, James Figg.

Jack Slack had many nicknames, including, rather unimaginatively, the Norfolk Butcher, the Knight of the Cleaver (after his profession) and The Bruiser (for obvious reasons). A contemporary description of Slack describes him as 5ft 8½in tall, weighing almost 14 stone and 'compact [...] superior to the generality of men in strength and of excellent bottom'.

In 1743, Jack became Champion of Norfolk after winning three separate matches and five years later, he turned his back on butchery and moved to London to pursue his fighting. However, his reputation as a dirty fighter dogged his career; he was the first man to use the illegal rabbit punch to the back of the neck. He also gained a reputation for deliberately losing fights. Slack's boxing style was so successful that the term a 'slack 'un' was generally used in the profession to mean a smashing hit.

Jack Slack returned to his home county from time to time, taking on worthy opponents. One such contest took place on 29 July 1754 in Harleston, when Slack challenged the Frenchman Jean Pettit, who had previously exhibited himself in a circus as a strongman. The *London Evening Post* reported of the match:

Jack Slack, the Knight of the Cleaver.

Yesterday in the afternoon Slack and Pettit met and fought. At the first set-to, Pettit seized Slack by the throat, and held him up against the tails, and grain'd him so much as to make him turn extremely black. This continued for half a minute before Slack could break Pettit's hold; after which, for near ten minutes, Pettit kept fighting hard at Slack; when at length Slack clos'd with his antagonist, and gave him a severe fall; after that, a second and third.

After twenty-five minutes, Jack was declared the winner; Pettit had walked out of the ring after suffering a nasty blow under the ribs.

Six years later, Slack lost his heavyweight title to Bill Stevens in a bout in London. After this, he reportedly went back to being a butcher – a far less violent way to earn a living!

***

There is a white stone memorial in Beeston-next-Mileham churchyard to a man who is described, simply, as Champion of the World. Jem Mace was one of eight children born to the village blacksmith and his wife and is widely acknowledged to have been the father of modern boxing.

Like Jack Slack before him, Mace was originally a bare-knuckle fighter. Jem had left the family home as a teenager to join the circus, also earning a meagre living playing the violin outside pubs. At the age of 18 he found himself in Great Yarmouth, where he was attacked by three fishermen one day while tuning his violin. Jem successfully fought them off and one of the gathered spectators suggested that he could make a living from fighting.

By 1861, Jem Mace was the Heavyweight Champion of England but soon after he worked with the Marquis of Queensbury to promote the use of boxing gloves in fights. In 1867, gloves were made compulsory under the Queensbury Rules and Jem Mace travelled the world evangelising about this more civilised, less brutal and undoubtedly life-saving way of fighting.

QUEENS

Anne Boleyn is, perhaps, one of Norfolk's most famous daughters. She is believed to have been born in Blickling Hall, in the predecessor of the Jacobean house that stands today. Her father, Thomas, held the Blickling Estate until 1505.

On 19 May 1536, Anne met a grisly end at the hands of an executioner at the Tower of London on the command of her infamous husband, Henry VIII. She and her brother George were both found guilty of treason and beheaded, George meeting his fate two days before Anne.

It is not surprising, then, that Blickling is the scene of reported regular ghostly sightings. It is said that every year on 19 May, Anne Boleyn arrives at midnight (or some say, dusk) in a horse-drawn carriage driven by a headless coachman. The queen emerges dressed in a white dress stained with blood that drips from her severed head, which she is holding.

The ghost of George Boleyn has also been seen in Norfolk on the same night, with his headless corpse being dragged through the countryside by four headless horses. Not content with these spectral appearances, on the eve of 19 May each year, a ghostly apparition, said to be Anne and George's father, Thomas, appears driving four headless horses across twelve Norfolk bridges, including Aylsham, Oxnead and Wroxham, carrying his head under his arm.

Although most history books tell us that Anne Boleyn's remains were buried in the Chapel Royal of St Peter ad Vincula at the Tower of London, rumours persist that Anne's body was retrieved by her father, who then arranged for her reburial in Salle Church, in an unmarked spot near to the monumental brasses of her great-grandparents, Geoffrey and Alice Boleyn. In *Bentley's Miscellany*, a monthly illustrated magazine of which Charles Dickens was the editor for many years, the famous author writes this moving account of Thomas Boleyn bringing the body of his daughter to Salle:

What the Earl's thoughts and reflections were during the two hours he was unobservedly travelling by Aylsham and Cawston to Salle, it would not be difficult to divine. He had within a month lost a daughter and a son by the hand of the executioner – that son his only son – that daughter the Queen of England. Her name, besides, had been branded with infamy […] the bitter reflections of those two hours perhaps the better prepared the Earl for the solemn ceremonies that awaited his coming at Salle Church. He alighted there at Midnight. A few faithful servants bore the mangled remains of his daughter to the side of her tomb […] One priest was there, and the few candles that were lighted did no more than show the gloom in which they were shrouded. But all that could be done for the murdered queen was done – mass was said for the repose of her soul – De Profundis (Psalm 130) was chanted by those present – her remains were carefully lowered into the grave, where they now rest, and a black marble slab, without either inscription or initials, alone marked the spot which contains all that was mortal of Anne Boleyn.

Sadly, we don't know what sources Dickens drew on because other published accounts do not give this amount of detail, although others do assert that Anne's body was conveyed to Salle and buried near her ancestors. We have to remember that Charles Dickens was a master storyteller.

Nevertheless, it is said that every year, on the anniversary of her death, the black marble slab in Salle Church, under which the earthly remains of Anne are said to rest, is visited by a weeping hare that waits until the last chime of midnight before bounding down the aisle and disappearing in the shadows beneath the tower.

★★★

Is this the final resting place of a Queen of England? (Tony Scheuregger)

The reign of the only daughter of the ill-fated Anne Boleyn was to prove one of the longest of any English monarch. Elizabeth I acceded to the throne in 1558 following the death of her Catholic half-sister, Mary, and died at the grand old age (for the time) of 69. Among other things, Elizabeth's reign is remembered for the time of great adventurers and their exploration of parts of the globe hitherto unexplored or, at least, little explored.

History books generally credit Sir Walter Raleigh with having first brought tobacco to England from America. However, it is believed that this dubious honour may fall instead to Sir Ralph Lane, a mariner and soldier and former Governor of Virginia. At the time of the threat of invasion by the Spanish Armada in 1588, Lane was put in charge of the construction of defences along the Norfolk coast. Two defensive mounds were constructed at Great Yarmouth, a garrison of 1,000 men was prepared and the town fitted out a warship in readiness for such an invasion. Some other planned defences were never completed, although fortifications were erected at Weybourne and Cley.

The colonist and mathematician Thomas Harriot, a close friend of Raleigh, recorded on his return from Virginia with Ralph Lane in July 1586, 'We ourselves have tried their way of inhaling the smoke and have had many rare and wonderful proofs of the beneficial effects of this plant which to relate in detail would require a whole volume to itself'. It is impossible to think that Lane and Harriot would not have brought back some of this tobacco to England.

By the end of the first Elizabethan era, the habit of smoking this weed had caught on and was accepted at all levels of society. It was, however, not without its opponents, who included the Bishop of Norwich, Joseph Hall, who had called smoking an 'abject' custom. Queen Elizabeth's successor to the throne of England, James I, was also an enlightened opponent of smoking, describing it as 'loathsome to the eye, hatefull to the nose, harmefull to the braine, dangerous to the lung and, in the black stinking fume thereof, nearest resembling the horrible Stigian smoke of the pit that is bottomlesse'.

During her long reign, Elizabeth I survived several plots and rebellions aimed at removing her from power. These plots came from a number of quarters: from disgruntled noblemen and from Catholics at home and overseas. They were often funded by powerful leaders from abroad and posed a significant threat to Elizabeth's crown. The best known of these

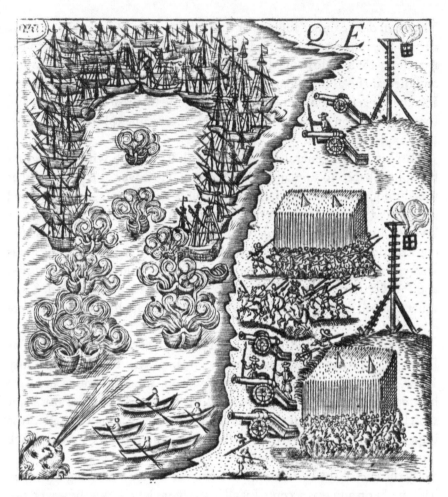

The English send fireships into the midst of the Spanish Armada in this contemporary woodcut.

were the Northern Rebellion, the Ridolfi Plot, the Throckmorton Plot and the Babington Plot, in which it was planned to replace Elizabeth with her cousin, Mary, Queen of Scots.

One of the lesser-known plots to assassinate Queen Elizabeth was to be launched on Midsummers Day in 1570 at the Harleston Fair. According to the Elizabethan chronicler John Stow, in the year leading up to this, certain factions in Norfolk had been gripped by rebellion against the queen and 'a conspiracy was made by certayne Gentlemen and other in the Countrey of Norffolke, whose purpose was on Midsomer day, at Harlestone faire, with sound of Trumpet and Drumme, to have reysed a number'. Robert Greene, an author and playwright contemporary with William Shakespeare, features the Harleston Plot in his stage comedy *Friar Bacon and Friar Bungay*, set mainly in north Suffolk near Harleston.

★★★

Iron Age Norfolk was occupied by the Iceni tribe, who were led by Queen Boudica. Her reputation as a formidable ruler is backed up by a surviving description of her by the Roman historian Tacitus, who wrote that she was 'very tall and severe [...] with] long red hair that fell to her hips'.

The village sign for the south Norfolk village of Quidenham features a modern painted-metal depiction of Boudica riding her two-horse chariot. She was chosen by residents to feature on this sign because legend has it that the Queen of the Iceni is buried in the parish at a place known as Viking's Mound.

Over the centuries, this mound on the north bank of the River Wittle has been incorrectly identified as a Bronze Age round barrow, a battlefield site and a Viking monument. The tumulus was known as the Bubberies in the nineteenth century, which lent weight to locals' assertion that this was a corruption of Boudica and thus pointed to her burial place. Sadly, more recent archaeological investigations have revealed the mound to be that of a twelfth-century motte-and-bailey castle built to guard the ford over the river.

The nearby village of Kenninghall has also, at some time in the past, laid claim to having been where Boudica held court, antiquarians having believed that the parish's name was a corruption of King's Hall.

A third location linked to Boudica, and another claiming to be the site of the queen's grave, is on Garboldisham Heath. Here, there are three large round barrows, the southernmost of these having been called Soldier's Hill since at least the 1850s. To date, this theory has not been disproved and it is certainly as good a candidate as any, given that Boudica's headquarters is believed to have been somewhere near the town of Thetford, not too far distant.

RED

The Norfolk coast has been threatened by the elements for centuries. The rate of sea erosion in the north of the county is still giving great cause for concern, not least among homeowners whose properties inch nearer to the edge of the cliffs each year.

Happisburgh has suffered from much erosion of the coastline, as evidenced from the sale deeds of what became Lighthouse Farm. When it was advertised for sale in 1790, it covered 280 acres but sixty-two years later, the land comprised just 176 acres.

The lighthouse at Happisburgh is undoubtedly the small village's most famous landmark and is the oldest working light in East Anglia. Originally called the High Light, this and another lighthouse, named the Low Light, were erected at Happisburgh by Trinity House following the loss of 600 men and seventy ships in the storms of 1789. The Low Light was threatened by coastal erosion and was withdrawn from service and demolished in 1883. This was also when the surviving lighthouse was first painted in its distinctive three red and two white stripes.

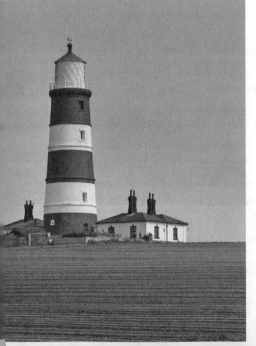

In 1987, Happisburgh was one of five lighthouses declared redundant by Trinity House. However, it was saved from deactivation by local residents, who established the Happisburgh Lighthouse Trust, becoming the only

The distinctive stripes of Happisburgh Lighthouse can be seen for miles around, both inland and out at sea. (Tony Scheuregger)

independent authority to run an operational light in Great Britain. Three years later, the lighthouse featured in an episode of the BBC TV programme *Challenge Anneka*, where the presenter Anneka Rice painted both the inside and the distinctive red and white stripes of the outside in just thirty-three hours. Unfortunately, the wrong sort of paint was reportedly used. It was last repainted in June 2018 at a cost of around £20,000 using specially mixed masonry paints donated by a paint company.

★★★

One of the ancient market squares in Norwich is Maddermarket, now dominated by the church of St John's, its churchyard and a recreation of an Elizabethan theatre created in the 1920s from a former Roman Catholic chapel. This area takes its name from one of the dyes that was traded here.

The use of dyers' madder (*Rubia tinctoria*) was almost certainly brought over by the sixteenth-century refugees from Flanders and it produced an attractive, permanent scarlet red colour. That said, a Norwich dyer called Ben Elder is usually credited with creating the so-called 'Norwich Red' dye with which the famous shawls produced in the city were coloured.

These shawls were first made in Norwich in the 1780s and the city led the way in producing shawls as soft as those from the Kashmir region of India, where they had originated. By the turn of the nineteenth century, there were twenty shawl manufacturers in Norwich and the industry was a major employer. Norwich weavers were highly skilled craftsmen with a long reputation for the excellent quality of their work. In 1825, a Mr Marten visited the city and recorded in this diary:

> We then walked about the large city & came by St Giles Church into Heigham, and called on Mr Grout who permitted us to go through his important Silk Manufactory. The works are in several floors and the winding twisting bobbins are by machinery moved by a beautiful 20-horsepower engine. These operations are watched and conducted by more than seventy females, some so young as 7 to 8 years of age. These are on foot from seven in the morning till eight in the evening watching the threads, repairing the broken & seeing that all go on well – occasionally supplying oil where wanted to prevent evil from friction. Only that they have half an hour to breakfast & an hour for dinner. And these little girls earn some 5 shillings, some 5 shillings/6d a week.

By 1870, madder was in great demand across the country and the plant was cultivated extensively in England, as well as in southern Europe. It grew best in a warm, bright climate in well-drained soils that were rich in humus. Madder could also be mixed with other dyes to produce permanent purple and black shades. Over time, of course, new synthetic dyes were invented, and the use of natural dyes fell away.

★★★

A memorial water trough in Cromer, now planted with flowers, seems to many a rather odd way to commemorate the man who first coined the term 'Poppyland', a word which describes so concisely and precisely the section of the north Norfolk coast stretching from Sheringham to Mundesley.

Clement Scott was a travel writer and journalist who published the first of his 'Poppyland' columns in *The Daily Telegraph* in August 1883, as letters written 'by a holidaymaker at a farmhouse by the sea'. This series and his later book, *Poppy-Land – Papers descriptive on the East Coast*, helped popularise this part of the county.

Scott wrote of cornfields swaying with red poppies while staying at Overstrand and it was in the churchyard at Sidestrand that he first penned the term in his poem, 'The Garden of Sleep', of which the first of the two verses reads:

On the grass of the cliff, at the edge of the steep,
God planted a garden – a garden of sleep!
'Neath the blue of sky, in the green of the corn,
It is there that the regal red poppies are born!
Brief days of desire, and long dreams of delight,
They are mine when Poppy-Land cometh in sight.
In music of distance, with eyes that are wet,
It is there I remember, and there I forget!
O! heart of my heart! where the poppies are born,
I am waiting for thee, in the hush of the corn.
Sleep! Sleep!
From the Cliff to the Deep!
Sleep, my Poppy-Land,
Sleep!

The railway line that first brought Scott and other Victorian tourists still operates as far as Sheringham. After that, it runs on to Holt as a heritage railway, which is run almost entirely by volunteers using vintage steam and diesel locomotives, today often referred to as the Poppy Line. One of the stations on this line, at Weybourne, is so photogenic and reminiscent of the great age of steam that it is often used for filming, most notably having been used in the 'Royal Train' episode in the *Dad's Army* series.

★★★

Near the centre of King's Lynn, there is a rather intriguing late medieval Gothic structure in a large park area known as the Walks. A simple plaque on the wall tells us that it is the 'Chapel of Our Lady of the Mount 1485', known as the Red Mount Chapel.

The octagonal, red-brick building sits atop a mound that is thought to be the remains of an early Norman motte-and-bailey fortification and it was built as a chapel of rest for pilgrims on their way to the holy shrine at Walsingham. However, over the centuries it has only been used as a religious building for fifty years or so.

After the Dissolution of the Monasteries, the chapel became the property of the town council. During the Civil War, it was used to store eighteen barrels of gunpowder and it is thought that during the Great Plague of 1665, the chapel doubled as a charnel house where the remains of the plague victims were kept.

In the following century, Red Mount Chapel housed horses before being repaired as an observatory for students of navigation. This English Heritage Grade I listed building narrowly avoided being destroyed by a German bomb that fell in the Walks in 1942. It was fully restored in 2008, thanks to a grant from the Heritage Lottery Fund and is now open to members of the public on certain days during the summer.

RING

Bells are among the oldest musical instruments in the world and were probably first cast in China more than 5,000 years ago. Bellringing has been associated with churches and Christian worship for around 1,500 years and many churches in Britain were built to include a tower that houses a ring of bells.

The Saxon, round-towered church of Aslacton has a remarkable set of fine bells, the oldest in Norfolk. They date from the early seventeenth century and are also the oldest complete ring by a single bellfounder. They are also unique in that they ring in an anticlockwise direction.

Aslacton's bells were cast in the foundry of William Brend of Norwich. Brend, along with his fellow bellfounders in the city, would have been members of one of the many guilds.

Back in 1194, Richard I had granted Norwich the right to self-government and, from this time on, the city authorities regulated the lives and livelihoods of its inhabitants. In 1404, a royal charter established a merchant guild, whereby all trades and occupations in Norwich were controlled by an elected council of freemen. Each trade had its own guild, which regulated the apprenticeship of boys to the craft and eventual acceptance by them as master craftsmen. Most guilds took fees from members, which were then spent on supporting those tradesmen who were out of work or retired.

As well as the ring of bells at Aslacton, there are two more sets of William Brend's bells in Norfolk – in St Peter, Repps, and at Claxton. These two sets comprise just three bells, as opposed to the five at Aslacton. The heaviest surviving William Brend bell, weighing in at over 800kg, is in Hingham Church.

***

The Church of St Nicholas, North Walsham, is one of Britain's largest parish churches. In the fourteenth century, the town was one of the main centres in the county for the weaving trade, thanks to the immigrant Flemish master weavers.

It was at this time that the church was rebuilt on a grand scale. It was some 164ft long with a tower 147ft high, one of the tallest in Norfolk. It is said that the North Walsham folk then added a lead-covered spire, adding a further 33ft to the overall height, purely to outdo the 158ft tower at Cromer.

On the morning of Saturday, 16 May 1724, however, St Nicholas' crowning glory came crashing down to the ground. The vicar, Thomas Jeffrey, noted the following in the parish register, 'Memorandum May 16. Between nine and ten o'clock in the forenoon on the Sat. fell down the north and south sides of the steeple and no person man woman nor child we hear of yet getting any mischief thereby. Thanks to be to God for this goodness therein.'

Apparently, the only person injured was a local doctor who was walking through the churchyard at that time. Luckily, his only injury was a cut to the ankle from a flying flint. It is highly likely that activity at the church the previous day contributed directly to the catastrophe. The bells in the tower had been rung for several hours for the Ascensiontide Fair, causing the structure to vibrate.

The tower and steeple were not rebuilt and, once open to the elements, the fabric of the building deteriorated further. At 6 p.m. on Wednesday, 17 February 1836, heavy gales brought down the north segment of the ruined tower, sending a tremor like an earthquake through the town. The remaining east belfry wall was later dismantled to a reduced height as a safety precaution.

Three years later, two men were brought before the Norfolk Assizes charged with stealing one of the bells from the collapsed North Walsham church tower. A further man, their accomplice, turned Queen's Evidence and told the court that the trio had taken the bell away in a cart, broken it up and tried to sell the metal for scrap.

St Nicholas' church tower was never rebuilt and is today a prominent landmark in North Walsham. As Nikolaus Pevsner in his Norfolk volume of *The Buildings of England* observes, 'it looks as decorative enough as a consolidated crag dominating the town'.

★★★

In the churchyard of St Nicholas at Woodrising, near Dereham, there is a dear little low, thatched building which is Grade II listed. It was probably constructed in the nineteenth century but reuses a late-medieval bell frame from the now ruinous tower of the church. It houses a single bell, which is rung on special occasions. The tower collapsed in the early eighteenth century and was, like many others, never rebuilt.

Inside the church is a tomb resplendent with a full-size alabaster effigy of Sir Richard Southwell of nearby Woodrising Hall. He died in 1563 and was succeeded as lord of the manor by his son, Robert. In 1578, Elizabeth I made a summer progress to East Anglia. She enjoyed hospitality from several titled gentlemen, including Sir Robert Southwell.

The thatched roof of Woodrising's bell cage almost completely hides its medieval frame. (George Plunkett)

Elizabeth's first overnight stop after her departure from Norwich, on her way back to London, was at Kimberley. From there, she travelled only a few miles to Woodrising, where she stayed for two nights.

Surviving documents give an insight into the huge logistical exercise involved in ensuring that the queen's party had enough to eat, as well as adequate supplies in order to carry out business. A farm at the nearby village of Letton sent butter and milk to Woodrising and the manor at Shipdham, a few miles away, contributed wax for document seals costing 8 shillings, wheat at 10 shillings and 8 pence, and oats for the horses costing 4 shillings and 6 pence.

The Shipdham churchwarden's accounts covering the time of the queen's visit record the payment of 8 pennies-worth of bread and drink for the bellringers who rang for the monarch. Although Woodrising is not within earshot of Shipdham, it seems likely that she went hunting in the nearby deer park and so the townsfolk of Shipdham thought they would play it safe by ringing their peal of bells in case the queen was able to hear them!

★★★

The village of Martham lies not too far distant from the North Sea coast of Norfolk and boasts a church much grander than others in the area. Indeed, from the top of the tower, you can see at least a dozen other churches. One of the bells in the tower of St Mary the Virgin bears the name Christopher Burraway, who died in 1730 and was one of the churchwardens, as well as a prominent member of the parish.

A visitor to Martham Church, therefore, might be surprised to read the epitaphs chiselled into one of two grave slabs that now lean against the south wall inside the building. They once lay on the floor of the nave and while one is relatively innocuous – it records the demise of Christopher Burraway, aged 59 – the other is for his wife, who died the year before Christopher and certainly raises an eyebrow or two. It reads, 'And there lyes Alice, who by hir Life was my Sister, my Mistres, my Mother and my Wife.'

This is, as you can see, quite a shocking statement, which obviously has attracted much attention since its original installation in the church. In 1851, the journal *Notes and Queries* published an article that sought to explain this enigmatic inscription. It stated that Christopher Burraway was the outcome of an incestuous relationship between a father and his daughter.

The baby had been placed in the Foundling Hospital and when he came of age, travelled to Martham and was hired by his own mother as a farm steward, neither knowing who the other was. In time, the two fell in love and married, thus Alice became his mother, sister, mistress and wife.

However, Alice eventually recognised a distinctive birth mark on his shoulder and realised that Christopher was her son. She was so horror-stricken that she died.

In reality, however, more recent research on the couple has revealed that there is little foundation for this story, although some elements of it are based on truth. In essence, Alice was married three times in total and her second husband, Gregory Johnson, was the widower of Christopher's mother, Mary, whom Mary had married after Christopher's father had died. Work that one out if you can!

STONES

The Priory of St Mary in the Meadow at Beeston Regis was founded in 1216 for a small community of just four ordained canons of the Order of Peterstone, which followed the rule of St Augustine. The Order of Peterstone was a small and rather mysterious religious order but one of their important roles was to act as parish priests for nearby churches.

The priory was not without its moments of trouble. In 1317, John de Walsam, one of the canons, had a serious row with the Bishop of Norwich resulting in de Walsam attacking the bishop with a sword and wounding him.

Like other religious houses, it was dissolved during the reign of

Henry VIII, one of the priory buildings being turned into a house and other parts left to go to ruin. Along with many other stones from the ruined priory were two large boulders that stood either side of a footpath leading through the grounds to a freshwater pond. According to a local tale, in the late 1930s, there were reports of a hooded grey ghost that would hide behind one of the two boulders and leap out at passers-by at sunset.

James Reynold's gravestone at All Saints, Beeston. (Tony Scheuregger)

One of the local farmers, James Reynolds, used to drive his horse and cart along this pathway and had had some close encounters with the ghost, who had tried to grab the horse's reins, spooking the animal. So, to stop the spectre from hiding behind the stone, Reynolds ordered that it be laid down upon his grave after his death. James Reynolds died in 1941 and, in accordance with his wishes, the boulder was used as his gravestone in the churchyard at All Saints, Beeston. The grey ghost was apparently never seen again.

★★★

Just off the road to Holt in Cawston, next to the former Woodrow Inn (now a garage) lies a patch of land with a Portland stone column at its centre. It is the smallest property in Norfolk owned by the National Trust and was presented to the charity in 1964.

This stone pedestal, inscribed with the initials 'HH', is topped by a stone urn and a nearby plaque explains:

> This urn commemorates the duel fought on the 20th of August 1698 between Sir Henry Hobart of Blickling Hall and Oliver Le Neve of Great Witchingham Hall. Their quarrel arose from words spoken in the heat of an election. Hobart was mortally wounded, and died at Blickling next day. Le Neve fled to Holland, but returned later, stood his trial and was acquitted.

Henry Hobart had represented King's Lynn in the last Parliament of Charles II and supported the revolution against James II. However, in 1698, Hobart failed to get re-elected. Rumours reached Blickling, however, that Oliver Le Neve had been spreading rumours that questioned Hobart's bravery and loyalty during his time campaigning for William III in Ireland.

Although Le Neve denied the accusation, Hobart publicly declared in the market square at Reepham that Le Neve had cost him the election. With neither party willing to back down, an appointment was made for a duel on 20 August 1698, even though duels had been technically illegal since 1614.

Hobart and Le Neve both rode from their respective country estates to a spot midway between the two on Cawston Heath. Henry Hobart was reportedly the better swordsman and wounded his opponent in the arm. Sir Henry's weapon, though, became caught in Le Neve's clothing and this allowed Le Neve to thrust his sword deep into his rival's stomach. Sir Henry Hobart died from his wounds the following day, back at Blickling Hall. His widow erected the memorial stone plinth and urn on the exact site of Hobart's fatal wounding, which also marks the spot of the last duel to have been held in Norfolk.

★★★

Norfolk folk are used to the sight of round towers on their churches: people who live elsewhere in the country are, arguably, not so familiar with these. Of the 180-odd churches with round towers in Britain (including those in ruins), most of these are in East Anglia and nearly three quarters are in Norfolk. Suffolk comes in second with a mere forty-two compared with Norfolk's 126. So, why did people in Norfolk choose to construct a round rather than square tower?

In fact, nobody really knows the answer but there are experts who have put forward several theories. The most popular possible reason is that they were relatively easy to build with the materials available locally where stone was hard to come by but flint was in plentiful supply. Flint is

The Norman round tower of St Mary, Surlingham, had an octagonal bell cage added in the sixteenth century. (Tony Scheuregger)

relatively small and has irregularly shaped pieces that cannot be as easily cut or worked as stone. When set into mortar, flint can create attractive patterns. However, this technique does not lend itself to making corners where quoins (or cornerstones) are needed. While a round tower made of flint may have been easier to build, it was quite a skilled job to position it next to the straight wall of the main body of the church.

St Mary's Church, Beachamwell, near Swaffham, is recorded in the Domesday Book and its round tower probably dates from Saxon times, albeit with later additions, including an octagonal belfry dating from the 1300s. As well as flint, those building the tower also used stone surrounds for the windows.

Beachamwell is also one of several churches in Norfolk to boast a magnificent thatched roof, that was, at least, until disaster struck on 2 February 2022. A major programme of building work had started just a week before this and was aimed at replacing previously stolen lead from the roof of the south aisle, as well as a partial rethatching of the roof covering the nave and chancel. It is thought that a spark from a workman's tool started a catastrophic blaze that destroyed the entire thatched roof and scorched the stonework. Smoke and water damage (from the firefighters' attempts to rescue the church) also left the building in a perilous state of repair.

Happily, however, due to the determined efforts of parishioners, the Grade I listed church has been deemed to be able to be restored. The first phase of the lengthy project, to stabilise the remaining structure and to remove the debris from the site, was already under way by the end of 2022.

★★★

In the graveyard of the Great Yarmouth parish of St Nicholas there is a remarkable grave marker that tells, in graphic detail, how the master of a ship staved off an attack by pirates off the coast at Great Yarmouth. The pirate ship was led by a notorious pirate named Daniel Fall, who had been terrorising ships along the East Anglian coastline since November 1780. Fall was described in the local press at the time as a smuggler and captain of a large privateer. The gravestone reads:

> To the memory of David Bartleman Master of the Brig Alexander and Margaret of North Shields who on the 31st of Jan 1781 on the Norfolk Coast with only three 3 pounders and ten Men and Boys nobly defended

himself against a Cutter carrying eighteen 4 pounders and upwards of a Hundred Men commanded by the notorious English Pirate Fall, and fairly beat him off. Two hours after the enemy came down upon him again. When totally disabled his Mate Daniel MacAuley, expiring with the loss of blood and himself dangerously wounded he was obliged to strike and ransome. He brought his shattered Vessel into Yarmouth with more than the Honours of a Conqueror and died here in consequence of his wounds on the 14th of February following in the 25th Year of his Age. To commemorate the Gallantry of his Son, the Bravery of his faithful Mate and at the same time Mark the Infamy of a Savage Pirate his afflicted father Alexander Bartleman has ordered this Stone to be erected over his Honourable Grave.

The epitaph underneath this sad but heroic tale reads, 'His Foe tho' strong was infamous (the foe of human kind) a manly indignation Fired his breast thank God my son has done his duty.'

This incident prompted the Mayor of Great Yarmouth to write an angry letter to the Admiralty in London complaining that they were not even willing to send a single warship to defend the Norfolk coast. Despite this loss of life, it was reported in April 1782 that Daniel Fall was taking his piracy to the Irish Sea and was, thankfully, not heard of again on the east coast.

★★★

It was the Romans who first instituted a system of milestones in Britain, so they could track their progress on the imperial roads they had constructed. These early milestones were cylindrical and were probably placed every thousandth double-step. The Latin for thousand is *mille* and the distance between each of these stones was 1,618 yards – today's standard British mile is 1,760 yards.

In the eighteenth century, when road travel was becoming vital for industry and communications, Turnpike Trusts were set up by Acts of Parliament to manage stretches of road and to ensure the upkeep of the main highways. From 1767, milestones were compulsory on all such roads, not only to inform travellers of direction and distances, but to help coaches keep to schedule. The distances were also used to calculate postal charges before the uniform postal rate was introduced in 1840.

The unusual milestone in Holt has stood in two previous locations. (George Plunkett)

Most early milestones were regular, low stone pillars with the name of the next main town carved into it, together with the number of miles to that particular destination. In Holt, a rather more unusual milestone is to be found at one end of the High Street. It is a tall, square pillar with a carved stone pineapple finial. It dates from the mid-eighteenth century and is said to have been moved from Melton Constable Hall and was apparently one of a pair of gateposts at the entrance to the estate.

Why and how they were removed remains a mystery, but one ended up in Holt and the other in Dereham. Each one had the distances to various places carved into the stonework on one side. In June 1940, with Britain at war with Germany, the government decreed that all place names should be hidden or removed to impede the enemy in case of invasion.

The authorities in Holt simply whitewashed out the writing. The Dereham folk, however, decided to throw their milestone down a well, where it remains to this day.

The lettering on the Holt milestone was restored some time after the end of the war. This obelisk, as it is known locally, stands close to another curious piece of street furniture called Blind Sam. This is a lantern that was manufactured for Queen Victoria's Golden Jubilee in 1887 and originally stood in Holt's Market Place. It provided light for the square and was powered by the town's own gas supply. It also provided drinking water from two fountains at its base. Because the gas supply was a little sporadic and therefore the lantern was, more often than not, dark, it earned its nickname, Blind Sam. When the war memorial was erected in the Market Place in 1921, the redundant light was moved to its present location.

STRIKE

The undoubted star of the show in Norfolk's capital, Norwich, is the Anglican cathedral. It was founded in 1096 by Herbert de Losinga and much of the cathedral and surrounding monastic buildings we see today were completed before his death in 1119. It is the largest building in East Anglia and the cathedral's spire, measuring 96m, is the second tallest (after that of Salisbury Cathedral) and is, depending on the source you consult, the third or fourth spire to have been built.

The original spire was constructed in wood and although it survived a lightning strike in June 1271, it was reportedly burned down by rioters in 1272. This was replaced by another wooden structure, which was then destroyed by a hurricane in 1362 and caused the spire to be rebuilt once again. A further wooden spire survived another 101 years until it, too, was destroyed by fire, following a lightning strike. Following this disaster, the bishop ordered the building of a new spire constructed from brick faced with stone, which was completed in the 1480s and it is this spire we see today.

Along with Norwich Cathedral, St Mary's Church at Erpingham vies for top spot as the most accident-prone place of worship in Norfolk! On 4 July 1665, in Norwich, a broadsheet (an early form of tabloid newspaper) was published that tells of a thunderstorm in Norwich and the surrounding area accompanied by great balls of lightning. According to the writer of the broadsheet, one of the balls of lightning struck the medieval church in Erpingham, destroying the porch and entering the church during a service.

The story continues, 'Mr Hobbs being in the pulpit, saw the men fall some one way, and some another, in such manner that he thought they had been all struck dead. It past towards the chancel, and brake; upon which the church was as if it been all of a fire.' One worshipper was left lame 'about the top of his thigh in the groyn, is round red place, and down from that about the breadth of a finger, a red streak to his foot, which is very painfull, and his stockin on the inside is seared, but not without'.

This was not the only catastrophe to befall the church. In 1721, one of the four statues standing at the corners of the tower fell during another service as a result of a storm that 'surprised the congregation; killed one and stupefied two others although they later recovered'. Barely 100 or so years after this fatal incident, part of the tower fell through the roof, destroying the baptismal font and then, in April 1888, the tower was once again struck by lightning, sending several large stones through the church roof. Happily, quieter times have returned to St Mary's, although perhaps today's parishioners keep their ears open for sounds of thunder when they kneel at prayer …

★★★

In 1984, in a small village not far from Diss, the first of what has now become an annual rally was held to commemorate the seventieth anniversary of the longest strike in British history. This strike, however, was not staged by miners but by minors – schoolchildren in Burston. On 1 April 1914, sixty-six children marched out of their local school and paraded around the village with cards hanging around their necks saying, 'We want our teachers back'. The banner at the head of the march carried just one word, 'justice', and the boycott of the council school in Burston lasted for over twenty-five years. The justice the schoolchildren were demanding was for the reinstatement of their teachers, Tom Higdon and his wife Annie, who had been sacked by the authorities.

The stone blocks on the front of Burston Strike School carry the subscribers' names. (Tony Scheuregger)

The Higdons had courted controversy before when they were both teaching at Wood Dalling School. The couple were Christian Socialists, who had objected to the poor conditions at the school, as well as complaining about employment of children by local farmers, which was hindering the scholars' education.

Tensions had run high, and the Norfolk Education Committee had found Tom and Annie Higdon alternative employment in Burston, away from any trouble, or so they thought. Unfortunately, Tom and Annie appear to have found exactly the same causes for concern in the rural community at Burston and they found themselves at odds with the school's managers, headed by the local rector. The Higdons were dismissed from their jobs in April 1914 based on reported abuse of some of the children, allegations many children and parents found difficult to believe.

The striking pupils never returned to their council school, instead, at first, being taught on the village green by Annie and Tom Higson. This alternative schooling maintained a complete timetable and had the full support of the parents, and ultimately the authorities found they could not compel the children to attend the official school. News of the school strike soon spread across the country and there were regular visits to Burston by supporters and speakers.

A national appeal was launched, and as a result of donations given by trade unions, the Independent Labour Party and Co-operative Societies, a new school was built that was opened on 13 May 1917. At the opening, the pupil leader of the 1914 demonstration, Violet Potter, declared, 'with joy and thankfulness I declare this school open to be forever a School of Freedom'. The Burston Strike School continued, under Mrs Higdon's leadership, to teach local children until 1939, when Mr Higdon died. The building is still there and now houses a museum telling the story of this amazing episode in British school history.

T

TURNIPS

Today, the Royal Norfolk Show is much more than a mere agricultural show, boasting 700 trade stands, over 3,000 animals and a packed programme of events in the main arena. It is hosted by the Royal Norfolk Agricultural Association, which aims to promote the image, understanding and prosperity of agriculture and the countryside. The annual show has been running every year since the charity was formed in 1847 and attracts visitors from every part of the country, as well as from overseas.

This association, however, was not the first to hold such large-scale agricultural events. Thomas William Coke – also known as Coke of Norfolk – was a farming pioneer who inherited the large estate of Holkham Hall in 1776. Coke embarked on an extensive remodelling and reorganisation of the parkland, centred around farming. It was a time when agricultural innovation was fashionable, and he encouraged the invention of new machines to speed up and improve crop management and livestock rearing.

Coke of Norfolk's annual, three-day Sheep Shearings at Holkham became the highlight of the agricultural year for farmers in Norfolk and those from further afield. New inventions were exhibited and forward-thinking ideas on all aspects of farming were discussed and disseminated. Coke introduced the Scottish turnip to his estate, as it had reportedly more flavour and was less watery than the native Norfolk turnip.

It is not surprising, then, that at his Sheep Shearings in 1810, one remarkable invention demonstrated was a turnip fumigating machine. It was a two-wheeled contraption that worked a pair of bellows. When the machine was pushed over the land and the wheels turned, the bellows blew air into an iron cylinder filled with burning sulphur and sawdust, which was distributed onto the ground through the perforations in the cylinder. The mixture supposedly suffocated and killed the turnip flies.

★★★

A century earlier, another member of the Norfolk aristocracy had made a name for himself in the field of agriculture. He is best known to schoolchildren as 'Turnip Townshend', who lived at Raynham Hall.

Charles 2nd Viscount Townshend was educated at Eton College and Cambridge University before taking his seat in the House of Lords in 1687. Townshend held several roles during his active political career, including Lord President of the Council and Secretary of State for the Northern Department. On his retirement from politics in 1730, Viscount Townshend played a key role in the British Agricultural Revolution, a period in which domestic agricultural output grew faster than the population.

His major contribution, which earned him his nickname, was promoting the adoption of the Norfolk four-course system. This dramatically improved productivity of the land for fodder crops. Wheat was grown in the first year, turnips in the second, followed by barley (with clover and ryegrass under sown) in the third. The clover and ryegrass were grazed or cut for feed in the fourth year. The turnips were used for feeding cattle and sheep in the winter months. When the sheep grazed the fields, their waste fertilised the soil, promoting heavier cereal yields in following years.

During periods spent overseas as a politician, Townshend had observed the way turnips were grown in Europe. He imported Continental turnip seeds and grew these stronger varieties in favour of the English plants. They were planted using the new horse-drawn seed drill that had recently been invented by Jethro Tull, another farming pioneer. This innovation allowed the economical planting of seeds in neat rows at the correct depth and spacing.

The Raynham Hall Estate in the twenty-first century, owned by the present Marquess and Marchioness Townshend, is still leading the way in adopting cutting-edge technologies, not only in agriculture but also in architecture and science. In 2015, a large solar farm was completed that serves over 12,000 homes with electricity. The same year, an anaerobic digestor was commissioned on the estate and generates biogas from agricultural crops and farm waste.

The turnip is, perhaps, the vegetable most closely associated with Norfolk's past.

★★★

In September 1822, the *Norfolk Chronicle* carried an advertisement for the sale by auction of 'all the valuable live and dead farming stock, agricultural implements, dairy and brewing utensils, and part of the household furniture' of Mr Robert Paul of Starston Hall, who was retiring from business. The article then continued with a detailed rundown of his equipment and animals, showing that he practised a wide range of mixed farming.

This advert is not at all unusual and numerous columns in the local newspapers of the time featured similar auction notices. So, Robert Paul appears to be just one of the thousands of his chosen profession across the county. However, on his death in April 1827 in nearby Harleston we learn that Robert was quite a remarkable man.

The *Suffolk Chronicle*, in reporting his death, described him as 'a man of considerable genius, and universally esteemed for his honest and manly integrity', while the *Norfolk Chronicle* said that he was 'well known to agriculturalists for several ingenious inventions, and for his interesting enquiries into the natural history and habitudes of the turnip fly and wire worm'.

A further search of online newspapers revealed that on 5 May 1811, a letter to the *Norfolk Chronicle* from Robert Paul was published in full and details his newly invented method for destroying turnip fly by sowing decoy turnips to lure the unwary flies, as well as a home-made 'machine'. He concluded:

> If what I have said above should induce my brother agriculturalists to bring the fly trap into general use, I shall have great satisfaction in the reflection that the trouble and expense I have been at in bringing the machine to the state in which it now is, have not been uselessly employed, and I shall feel happy if any one more capable than myself should bring it to a still greater state of perfection.

TWINS

Several years ago, my father gave me a run of the *East Anglian Magazine*. I have avidly sought out missing numbers and now have a great collection, which provides endless fodder for my curious tales. I do find, however, that the facts of the articles in this magazine need constant checking for accuracy. One lovely story appears in the February 1976 issue, and I have yet to prove its veracity. Nevertheless, it is worth repeating here, albeit with that health warning.

There are identical twin headstones in the churchyard of Tivetshall St Margaret. Each stone has at the top a chiselled cherub holding a scythe and resting an elbow on an hourglass. When I say identical, they are in all respects, other than the cherubs mirror one another in stance.

It is said that the graves are those of two brothers by the name of Jolly who, for a wager of beer, competed against one another to see who could mow the fastest and longest in cutting down the corn in a 70-acre field at Hall Farm. On a hot day in August 1725, the Jolly brothers scythed until they both dropped down from exhaustion and died.

Sadly, the Tivetshall St Margaret parish registers do not back up this tale. A Thomas Jolly was buried on 31 August 1725, which suggests there is some element of truth in the story. However, there is no other male Jolly buried in this or subsequent years. Perhaps one of the brothers died and the other lived on, regretting that fateful day?

On 22 December 1725, the incumbent buried a 'Widow Jolly'. While we don't know for sure that this was the widow of Thomas, I like to think that these lovely twin headstones are those of a devoted man and wife and that they rest in peace together.

★★★

There is another wonderful legend, more widely known, attached to the twin churches of St Margaret's and St Mary's in the parish of Antingham. Both places of worship share the same churchyard and we are told that they were built by two sisters after whom the churches were named.

Similar stories abound in other parishes in Norfolk where there are (or were) two churches sharing the same graveyard – some dozen or so, in total. In fact, this phenomenon only occurs in East Anglia, with Norfolk possessing the most examples.

The atmospheric ruined tower of St Margaret's at Antingham stands in the same churchyard as St Mary's. (Tony Scheuregger)

The tale continues that these two sisters, who inherited equal shares in their father's manor, fell out with one another and therefore each built their own church. One of the sisters was a 'bad lot' and, as a result, her church fell into disrepair, as opposed to the good sister, whose church flourished.

While most of this story is fantasy, it may have a grain of truth. In the case of Antingham, the reason may have had something to do with divided lordship of manorial land in the medieval era. In others, perhaps one church simply became too small for the parishioners and so a second, larger one was built, leaving the first to become ruined.

A case of land division within a manor occurs at South Walsham, where the partially ruined St Lawrence sits next to St Mary's, which still welcomes congregations. Even though St Lawrence was burnt out in 1827, it continued distinct from St Mary's, with its own rector, until 1890. It took until 1986 for the twin parishes to be formally united. The tower of St Lawrence had split vertically, and the western side was still standing, until 1971, when a combination of lightning, high winds and a sonic boom brought it tumbling down. All that is now left of it is the chancel with a small nineteenth-century extension. The building has been carefully restored and now operates as a centre for the arts, hosting concerts, art exhibitions and community events.

UNDERGROUND

When we think of subterranean Norwich, many long-time residents will remember the astonishing sight of a double-decker bus having been swallowed up by a sinkhole in 1988. Since then, other holes have appeared on a regular basis across the city, mostly on the outskirts.

It is the chalk on which Norwich is built that makes it vulnerable to such occurrences. When rainwater flows into cracks in the chalk, it pushes the cracks further apart until a hole appears or until the top of the chalk collapses.

In one of crime writer Elly Griffith's Ruth Galloway novels, *The Chalk Pit*, the archaeologist investigates a set of boiled human bones in Norwich's web of underground tunnels. She discovers a vast community – the Underground – living in the network of old chalk-mining tunnels. From the Middle Ages through to the middle of the twentieth century, chalk and flint mines operated in the city. This building material was used to construct some of Norwich's iconic buildings such as the guildhall.

There are many stories of tunnels underneath Norwich, some running from the castle to locations such as the guildhall and the cathedral. Another tunnel is said to run from the castle to the former Benedictine nunnery, Carrow Priory, in which, apparently, a pig was once lost.

There are also rumours of smugglers' underground passages between Upper King Street and Pull's Ferry by the riverside. Other tunnels are said to run between some of the religious institutions and the pubs, including one from St Peter Mancroft Church to the nearby (but now demolished) White Swan Inn, said to have been used by priests.

In January 1644, Oliver Cromwell sent his army to Norwich to demand the surrender of a small group of Royalists, who he had heard to be at the Maid's Head Hotel. According to legend, as the Parliamentarians entered the hotel, the Royalists retreated through a secret tunnel, stretching steel ropes across the way behind them. Many of Cromwell's men and their horses were beheaded as they raced through the tunnel in pursuit. This story is used to explain the sound of ghostly hoofbeats that are heard emanating from under the ground around the Cathedral Close, especially about midnight near the end of January.

★★★

The chancel of All Saints Church at Narborough, near King's Lynn, has a splendid Jacobean monument to Sir Clement Spelman and his wife, boasting life-size effigies of the couple. Above them kneels their daughter along with a baby in a cot. The baby was the young Clement, who grew up to be Sir Clement Spelman, a justice of the peace.

He is not buried with his parents. His memorial stands on the opposite side of the chancel, where he stands, resplendent in his wig and robes, on a tall pedestal. It is believed that the statue was originally intended to have a more elaborate setting. It was to have been set within a richly carved niche with angels holding a laurel crown above his head and attendant figures of Time, gazing on an hourglass, and Death holding a dart. Why this detail was not incorporated in the final sculpture is unknown.

When the Victorians came to restore All Saints, they found Clement Spelman's monument to be unsafe and so preparations were made to reduce the height of the 2.5m pedestal to half its original dimension. In doing so, they discovered that Spelman had never been interred underground. Instead, his body was in his coffin, which was standing upright inside the pedestal.

Nikolaus Pevsner, in his Norfolk volume of *The Buildings of England*, explains that the pompous Spelman could not endure the thought of being trodden on after his death and so ordered his 'burial' to be above ground in this rather strange fashion. The restoration continued, and disregarding the long-dead judge's wishes, the coffin was moved and reburied under the floor in another part of the church and the pedestal duly shortened.

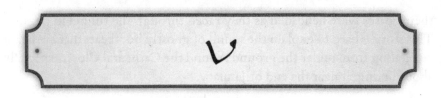

VICTORY

A visitor by road crossing the boundary into Norfolk is greeted by a proud sign announcing it as 'Nelson's County'. A bold and proud claim, which is backed up by Lord Horatio Nelson's words himself on being greeted by cheering crowds at Great Yarmouth after his victory at the Battle of the Nile, 'I am myself a Norfolk man and glory in being so'.

Those wanting to follow in the footsteps of the great admiral will no doubt start their tour in the village of Burnham Thorpe, where Nelson's father, Edmund, was the rector and where, in the Church of All Saints, the baby Horatio was baptised in 1758. When the church was restored in 1890 in honour of the parish's most famous son, the Admiralty donated wood from HMS *Victory*, from which the lectern, altar and rood screen were made.

A story is told of how, as a child, Nelson went off bird-nesting in Burnham Thorpe with some of his fellow village boys. Horatio, however, managed to wander off on his own. When he did not appear home for supper, his family set off in search for him and found him sitting on the far side of a river, which he had been unable to cross. On reaching the parsonage, his grandmother asked, 'Horatio, I wonder that hunger and fear did not drive you home', to which the young Nelson replied, 'Fear! I never saw fear – what is it?'

On 6 November 1800, Lord Nelson finally arrived in Britain after his famous victory in Egypt two years previously. He came ashore at Great Yarmouth and this report appeared in the rather curiously named, London-based newspaper, the *Porcupine*:

At Yarmouth, the instant he had landed, the mayor and corporation waited on him with the address and the freedom of the town. The infantry in the town paraded before the inn where he lodged, with their regimental band, firing *feux de joye* of musquetry and ordnance till midnight. The corporation in procession, with the respectable officers of the navy, went to church with Lord Nelson and Sir William and Lady Hamilton to join in thanksgiving. On leaving the town, the corps of cavalry unexpectedly drew up, saluted, and followed the carriage, not only to the town's end but to the boundary of the county.

What this report fails to mention are two amusing little anecdotes that emerged after Nelson's visit that day, bearing in mind that Nelson had already lost his right arm in the Battle of Santa Cruz de Tenerife.

At the swearing-in ceremony to receive the Freedom of the Borough of Great Yarmouth, the town clerk asked Lord Nelson to place a hand on the Bible, which he duly did with his remaining left hand. The official, however, had somehow not noticed the amputation and said to him, 'Your right hand, my Lord.' The hero replied witheringly, 'That is in Tenerife.'

The same day, Nelson and his entourage were taken by carriage to the Wrestlers Inn on Church Plain. The landlady, Mrs Suckling, asked whether she might be allowed the honour of renaming the pub the Nelson Arms, to which the great seaman retorted, 'That would be absurd, seeing that I have but one!'

Nelson's county was the first to honour Nelson after his death by erecting the first Nelson's Column on the South Denes at Great Yarmouth. In fact, it was originally conceived during his lifetime to commemorate his victory at the Nile but progress had been painfully slow, mainly in raising the necessary £10,000 needed to construct the pillar. When it was finally completed in 1819 – twenty-four years before its more famous twin in Trafalgar Square was built – the monument stood 144ft tall with 217 spiral steps inside the column leading to a viewing platform.

A statue of Britannia holding a trident and a laurel leaf tops the pedestal. Surprisingly, Britannia does not face seaward towards the scene of Lord Nelson's many victorious battles and there have been a few competing theories as to the reason for this. Some said that it was a pure mistake by the man who fixed the figure on the top and, when realising his mistake, he threw himself off the top in remorse. Others believe that the figure faces towards the ships sailing along the River Yare towards the sea, reminding them that Britannia rules the waves. However, the most enduring reason is that it faces inland in the direction of Nelson's birthplace at Burnham Thorpe.

At the base of the memorial there is an inscription in Latin, part of which translates as:

This great man Norfolk boasts her own, not only as born there of a respectable family, and as there having received his early education, but her own also in talents, manners and mind.

In May 1863, the local and national newspapers carried reports of a 'Frightful and fatal accident' at Nelson's monument in Yarmouth. The inquest into the death, which was covered word for word by the *Norfolk Chronicle,* concluded that a strolling singer called Charles Marsh was accidentally killed. He and fellow musician, Henry Wharton, had been drinking at the Monument Tavern and were therefore 'rather the worse for drink'.

It appears that they bet their fellow drinkers that they could climb the column, Marsh performing 'God Save the Queen' on his violin with Wharton accompanying him on the banjo. Having successfully arrived at the plinth at the top, Charles went on to mount the figure of Britannia, waving to the crowds gathered at the foot of the column. In preparing his descent, though, Marsh lost his grip on Britannia's trident, overbalanced and fell. On realising that his friend was plummeting to the ground, Wharton reported that he ran down the steps as hard as he could in order to overtake him before he could get to the bottom. What he thought he might have done to save Marsh, we don't know, but sadly, by the time he exited the monument, Wharton found his friend lying on the ground, dead.

Nelson's monument in Great Yarmouth once dominated the landscape.

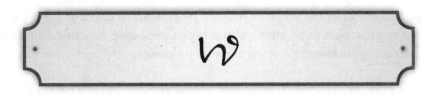

WAGERS

I lowly beg pardon and leave, for my taborer strikes up his Hunt's Up, I must to Norwich: Imagine noble Mistress, I am now setting from My Lord Mayor's, the hour about seven, the morning gloomy, the company many, my heart merry.

So, with these words to his patron Anne Fitton, the comic actor Will Kemp left London on the first Monday in Lent in February 1600. His extraordinary feat was to dance a Morris from the capital to Norwich, which was then England's second-most important city.

Kemp had left a company of actors called the Lord Chamberlain's Men the previous year, apparently after a falling out with the troupe, which included none other than William Shakespeare. In fact, it is thought that some of Shakespeare's comic roles were written specifically for Kemp to play, including Dogberry in *Much Ado About Nothing* and Peter in *Romeo and Juliet*.

The comic actor, or clown, had an important place in Shakespeare's plays and would be expected to improvise with song and dance, so Will Kemp was quite used to dancing. Nevertheless, a 110-odd mile Morris dance from London to Norwich was a serious undertaking. Naturally, he took overnight breaks along the way, and he completed the venture in just nine days of dancing.

Kemp's elaborate stunt was part of a wager he had with an unspecified number of individuals as to whether he could complete the epic dance. At every point on his journey to Norwich, Will Kemp was cheered on by crowds of well-wishers, and met the top brass in towns he passed through, including in Thetford, where Sir Edwin Rich gave the actor £5.

We know so much extraordinary detail about Kemp's exploits because shortly after he returned to London, he published his own account of the dance, entitled *Kemp's Nine Daies Wonder*. In it, he records how he received a spectacular welcome when he reached Norwich, the crush of the crowds being so great that in an attempt to escape the people, he caused a rather embarrassing incident involving a female onlooker:

> […] and coming unluckily in my way, as I was fetching a leap, it fell out that I set my foot on her skirts, the point either breaking or stretching, off fell her petticoat from her waist […] the poor wench was so ashamed that now had she her cheeks all coloured with scarlet I was sorry for her but on I went to the mayor's and deceived the people by leaping over the churchyard wall at St John's.

Although Will Kemp fulfilled his side of the bet, it is thought that he failed to collect all the money from his original backers. Kemp never returned to the stage and is thought to have died in 1603.

★★★

A rather eccentric man called Robert Skipper lived in Norfolk's capital city in the early nineteenth century. He was well-known, across the country and even on the Continent, as the Norfolk Pedestrian, for obvious reasons.

Skipper did not, however, just walk for pleasure or for his health. Instead, he appears to have undertaken these perambulations in an attempt to win bets. That said, Robert Skipper does not seem to have had much success. The *Norfolk Chronicle* tracked his progress on several occasions, including in July 1817 when the newspaper reported that Skipper had undertaken a wager to walk from Norwich to Thetford and back in twelve hours. According to the report, 'He walked 54 miles, but having only four minutes to perform the last mile, gave in.'

Later the same year, the Norwich Pedestrian attempted to walk 60 miles in twelve hours on the bowling green at the King's Head Inn in East Dereham. Sadly, 'he was so exhausted in the last two miles that he could not accomplish his task'.

Perhaps his lack of stamina led him to train harder because a year later, in September 1818, the *Norfolk Chronicle* reported that Robert had started out from St Stephen's Gate in Norwich on a mammoth 1,000-mile walk, which he aimed to complete in twenty days. Yet again, his efforts were thwarted when 'he relinquished the task on the ninth day in consequence of lameness'. Robert Skipper tried again in October 1821 but had to give up while walking his 190th mile 'in consequence of magisterial interference'.

Despite Skipper's constant failure to complete his challenges, it appears that it really does pay to keep on trying. A poster survives that details a walk Robert attempted on the other side of the Channel, which reads:

NOTICE. By permission of the authorities, the celebrated English pedestrian Robert Skipper, aged 41 years, is arrived in this town on his way to Paris, where he is to perform the unprecedented match of walking 1,000 miles in 1,000 successive half-hours. He intends to perform at Boulogne the Herculean Task of going on foot 100 miles in 20 hours, to commence at 12 o'clock next Monday night, and to finish at 8 o'clock on Tuesday evening; on a measured piece of ground of a half-mile, selected on the ramparts. And as this arduous undertaking is voluntary, he entirely trusts to the liberality of the Public. N.B. Two proper persons will be appointed to witness the just performance. Boulogne-sur-mer 13th of July 1827.

A handwritten note in ink appears on the bottom of the poster, which reads, 'Finished it within 23 minutes of 8 o'clock Tuesday evening 17th July 1827.' So, it seems that the Norwich Pedestrian was successful in the end!

★★★

Today, it is the sporting world that we most associate with betting and while we often wager some money on other things, for instance, the likelihood of a white Christmas, we don't hear much about gastronomic bets. Not so in the late eighteenth century, where these seemed rather more common. The following two extracts were gleaned from local newspapers dating from the 1770s and 1780s:

A young fellow engaged, for a trifling wager, to eat a shoulder of mutton of seven pounds weight for his supper at a public house at St Stephen's, Norwich. He was not confined to time, but in the space of something more than an hour, he devoured the whole except for about half a pound of fat, which notwithstanding his endeavours, his stomach rejected, and he was obliged to submit to the loss of his wager.

A cowkeeper in Norwich laid a wager lately that two cows in his possession eat 48 stone of turnips in 24 hours, which they accomplished in 22.

WHEELS

There is a rather curious iron wheel that sits, encased in glass, in the church at Long Stratton. It is 80cm in diameter and has eight spokes between which are large fleurs-de-lys (although one is missing). The only other decoration is the pattern of petals around the hub. This item was not merely to enhance the beauty of the church: it must have served some purpose.

The only other example in the country is in Yaxley Church in Suffolk and is very similar in design. Had it not been for the research of a Yaxley clergyman, Reverend W.H. Sewell, in the late-nineteenth century, we may have never known how these wheels were used. He discovered that the wheel would have been a

Long Stratton's Sexton's Wheel has lost one of its fleurs-de-lys.

common sight in medieval churches, and we can discover its purpose from Sewell's translation from the original Latin of these rhyming instructions, dating from 1559:

Besides they keep our Lady's fast at sundry solemn times
Instructed by a turning wheel, or as the lot assigns.
For every Sexton has a wheel that hangs for the view,
Marked roundabout with certain days, unto the Virgin due
Which holy through the year are kept, from whence hands down a thread,
Of length sufficient to be touched, and to be handled.
Now when that any servant of our Lady's comes here,
And seeks to have some certain day by lot for to appear,
The Sexton turns the wheel about, and bids the stander by
To hold the thread whereby he does the time and season try:
Wherein he ought to keep his fast, and every other thing,
That decent is or longing to our Lady's worshipping.

So, we learn that six marked threads were hung from the wheel and a parishioner would grasp one of these while the wheel was spinning. He or she would then be obliged to start their prayer and fasting on whichever of the six holy days dedicated to the Virgin Mary that thread represented. The wheel was looked after and spun by the parish officer responsible for the church building and churchyard, the sexton, hence its present-day name, the Sexton's Wheel.

★★★

The ancient town of Fakenham can boast royal origins that date back to the time of the Wars of the Roses. John of Gaunt, the third son of Edward III, who was the founder of the House of Lancaster, was given the Manor of Fakenham in 1377. The town's full name therefore is Fakenham Lancaster – a fact unknown to many, including some of its residents!

Fakenham commands a prominent position in the county and so would have been visited by pilgrims on their way to the holy shrine at Walsingham. It was also on the main coaching route to and from London. In the 1830s, the soon to be queen, Princess Victoria, visited Fakenham when her coach had to negotiate a ford through the River Wensum.

Unfortunately, her carriage became stuck in the ford and the monarch – who was not amused– vowed never to return unless a bridge was built. So, in 1833, a bridge was duly built using paupers from the nearby poor house to provide the labour. Despite this, and the fact the bridge over the river was named for Queen Victoria, she never returned to Fakenham.

★★★

Some forty years before the queen's visit, the Fakenham mail coach was at the centre of a rather strange occurrence involving two strongmen. In 1795, Ned Denny, known as the Norfolk Samson, and Seth Blowers, the Suffolk Giant, came up against one another to pull a coach with their respective noble backers inside. The start line was at the Crown Inn at Fakenham and they were supposed to finish at the Royal George Inn at Walsingham.

Ned Denny, who was pulling the mail coach, was within 10 yards of the finish when he fell and the coach ran on with Denny dead, still in his harness. Seth Blowers managed to stagger across the finish line just before collapsing. He died three days later.

★★★

An engraving depicting an eighteenth-century wheelwright's workshop.

A very rare survival stands on the village green at East Walton. It is a small yellow- and red-brick structure with a barrel-vaulted roof and a central chimney. Nearby, a circular iron plate gives the visitor a first clue as to the building's former use.

It was built in the mid-nineteenth century and is a wheelwright's oven. A tithe map of 1843 shows a forge just to the north of the oven, which was the blacksmith and wheelwright's premises.

The oven was used for heating the iron rims of the wheels for carts and carriages and could hold six tyres standing upright – three large and three smaller ones. Once a metal rim was heated, it would be removed from the oven and placed around the wooden wheel, which would sit flat in the circular plate. The hot metal would then be hammered against the wood and buckets of cold water, from a well on the green, were then thrown over it to cool the rim. This created a perfect iron-clad wheel.

The oven, certainly the only one of its kind in Norfolk and possibly in the country, was in use until around 1940. It was restored in 1977 and again in 1990.

WHITE

Norfolk seems to have several ghostly white ladies, but perhaps other counties have a similar number of curious spectres? This may well be the case, because since the Middle Ages, the appearance of such white ladies is said to go together with tragedies such as accidental death, murder or suicide often associated with unrequited love or betrayal.

In Old Catton, a suburban village of Norwich, there is a White Woman Lane, named for a spectre who has been seen for hundreds of years, drifting down the road in her wedding dress. There are several stories to explain this apparition.

One is that the daughter of a local squire fell in love with one of her father's coachmen, who lived on the opposite side of the road. The smitten young woman would steal out in the night to visit her lover. Inevitably, her father found out about the affair and sacked the coachman, who packed up and prepared to leave in the coach and horses. The distraught lady ran after him and slipped under the coach wheels, dying instantly.

Other tales suggest that the lady is the ill-fated wife of the Lord of Catton Old Hall, who died as a result of his cruelty. A variation on this story suggests that the lady was preparing to marry a lord but died the night before the ceremony.

The Shrieking Pits at Aylmerton are several hollows in the ground believed to be ancient iron-working pits. It is said that a weeping woman in white is seen moving from one pit to another, looking down into each one in turn and shrieking in anguish. Folklore tells us that the woman is looking for the lifeless body of her baby, who was killed by her jealous husband and thrown into one of the pits, because the husband was convinced that the child was not his.

Many of Norfolk's stately homes also have their fair share of ghosts and Wolterton Hall is one of these. The house was built by Horatio Walpole, the brother of the statesman Sir Robert Walpole in the first half of the eighteenth century and remained in the Walpole family until 2016.

Lady Dorothy Nevill, who wrote *Mannington and the Walpoles* in 1894, records that a white lady, who often appeared when some calamity was about the befall the family, had been seen by servants. The lady was said to be one of the Scamler family who had owned Wolterton before the Walpoles and whose tombs in the churchyard had been disturbed. Nevill also reports yet another lady who is believed to haunt the mansion:

In the drawing-room is a full-length portrait of Ambassador Horace Walpole. This gentleman formed part of a large picture comprising himself and wife and seven or eight children, some of which are represented as angels, apparently having died as babies. This picture was cut up and the portraits of the children given to different members of the family, whose descendants they are. The unhappy wife is said to haunt Wolterton seeking for her divided relatives.

Finally, there is the legendary white lady at St Mary's Church at Worstead, who was captured on film in 1975 by an unsuspecting couple who visited the church on Christmas Eve, when she is said to appear in the tower as the clock chimes midnight.

★★★

Before it was bypassed, the former White Hart Inn (currently the Scole Inn Hotel) was once ideally located on the main coaching routes leading across East Anglia from north to south and west to east. In fact, the village's name is a corruption of 'Score', thus called because was a score of miles (20) away from Ipswich, Bury St Edmunds, Thetford and Norwich.

At the height of the horse-drawn coaching era, the White Hart welcomed up to forty coaches a day, stabling the horses and providing food, drink and comfortable accommodation for weary travellers. In its early days as an inn, on 27 September 1671, it was even visited by a monarch, albeit briefly and at the local squire's expense (!), as the local parish register records, 'King Charles the Second passed through Scoale [sic] in his progress to Yarmouth and brake his fast at the White Hart at the charge of the Right Honourable Lord Cornwallis.'

The White Hart is also said to have witnessed an unusual sight in the 1780s when the highwayman John Belcher rode up the main staircase on his horse to evade officers of the law. Some histories also offer up the fact that one of the bedrooms housed a bed capable of accommodating thirty to forty people with their feet towards the centre. It also boasts that two of the magnificent fireplaces in the bar are reputedly the largest in East Anglia.

However, the main feature for which the inn was once famous disappeared completely in the mid-nineteenth century. This was a large, elaborate sign that straddled the turnpike road. Apart from a White Hart, it featured carved figures of Diana, Actaeon, Neptune, Father Time, Justice,

The spectacular sign of the White Hart which once straddled one of the county's main coaching routes at Scole.

lions and several other figures, one of which acted as a weathervane. The cost of making the sign, in 1655 when the inn was built, was over £1,000 and it was considered by Sir Thomas Browne of Norwich to be 'the noblest signpost in England'.

★★★

The small parish of Langley with Hardley, about 12 miles south-east of Norwich in the Yare Valley, is, by all accounts, a peaceful and law-abiding village. Back in the fifteenth century, however, all was less than calm and in the unlikeliest of places – Langley Abbey.

This once large and magnificent range of monastic buildings was founded in 1195 by the Lord of Langley, Sir Robert Fitzroger. It was run by the Premonstratensian order of canons who, because of the colour of the habits they wore, were known as the White Canons.

Along with their daily duties and the religious services they held in the abbey itself, they also took on the role of parish priests for the surrounding villages. In the early 1300s, the presiding Abbot of Langley was accused of embezzling the £200 tax money collected from local residents in aid of the Crusades.

Then, in the latter part of the 1400s, Bishop Richard Redmond, the visiting Commissary General of the Premonstratensian order, recorded a series of misdemeanours with which he had to deal. In 1478, Canon Thomas Russell was sentenced to forty days' penance and was banished to Tichfield for three years for 'evil living'. Four years later, the abbot was reported as being guilty of squandering the abbey's money on his own lifestyle. The bishop noted, 'Common taverns near the monastery were not to be visited.'

In 1488, under a new abbot, Walter Alpe, it was noted that vows of silence were being ignored and 'there should be no hunting or fishing at night and no illicit desertion'. Alpe did not seem to mend his ways because three years after being reprimanded, he was charged with being 'wanting in self-restraint and with dilapidation'. Finally, in the early 1500s, Walter Alpe was warned that he should 'not be seen in association with the woman who had been named'. Abbot Walter Alpe resigned shortly afterwards.

When Langley Abbey was finally dissolved in 1536, only six White Canons remained. Much of the abbey was demolished and used for building materials elsewhere in the area.

WRINKLES

In 1990, an amazing discovery was made that put Norfolk firmly on the Ice Age map. After a winter storm, locals at West Runton found some large, well-preserved bones had been partially exposed at the base of the cliff face. Over the next two years, more bones from the same animal were discovered after other storms.

When the bones were fully excavated, an almost complete skeleton emerged. These were identified as belonging to a species called *Mammuthus trogontherii*, more commonly known as the steppe mammoth. This was probably the largest species of its kind ever to have lived on earth.

The West Runton mammoth weighed 10 tonnes and measured around 4m at the shoulder. From teeth marks on some of the bones, experts were able to tell that the mammoth had been savaged by spotted hyenas. They were also able to tell that the mammoth was male because of the shape of the pelvis. Pathologists examined the skeleton and found that he had a diseased and deformed right knee. This may well have contributed to his early death.

By examining the wear on his teeth, scientists established that the mammoth was in his forties when he died – most would normally have lived into their sixties. To date, it is the oldest mammoth skeleton ever to be found in this country, having lived between 600,000 and 700,000 years ago.

For two decades or so, the West Runton mammoth was thought to have roamed what is now Norfolk at a time long before the first humans appeared here. However, in 2013, spring and winter storms uncovered a series of fossil footprints some 30km along the coast at Happisburgh. Remarkably, archaeologists were able to demonstrate that these prints were left by a group of at least five people, including an adult male, females and possibly children. The footprints provide evidence that these people were here some 950,000 years ago, long before the mammoth!

The West Runton mammoth weighed 10 tonnes.

***

There are more than 3,000 village signs in Britain, but Norfolk boasts the largest roadside gallery in any one county with well over 500. More importantly, though, village signs originated in Norfolk and first sprang up in the early years of the twentieth century.

The Prince of Wales, later to become Edward VII, commissioned the Princess Alexandra School of Carving to make signs for villages on the Sandringham Estate as a means of fostering community spirit and identity. It also helped early motorists to find places of interest. Edward VII's son, George V, also championed the trend, erecting a further three on the estate.

Although these first signs have been restored and repainted many times, they still bear the date 1912. One of these is at Wolferton and displays two dates: 1912 and 2012. The first indicates the date the sign was first unveiled, the year after George VII was crowned. The second was to celebrate the Diamond Jubilee of Elizabeth II.

In 1920, at a speech he gave at the Royal Academy, the king described the village sign as 'a welcome guide to the visitor in a strange land'. He told the audience, 'The name of many a village would offer scope for the wit and humour of the artist. In the neighbourhood of Sandringham village signs have been introduced with considerable success.' The idea quickly caught on, helped along by a village signs competition put on by the *Daily Mail*.

Today, village signs come in all manner of shapes and sizes, and most depict or represent local people, places and happenings. There are those that show famous clergymen and others that feature windmills, past and present.

The materials with which our village signs are constructed also vary greatly. Many, including the older ones, are carved wooden signs and, remarkably, quite a few are the work of the same craftsman.

Harry Carter of Swaffham first turned his hand to making such signs in 1929 with one for his home town. Another of his, however, comes with a warning that not all village signs depict anything remotely resembling part of their local history. In August 1956, an oak sign created by Harry Carter was unveiled in the Norwich suburb of Eaton. It shows a white elephant holding a barrel in its curled-up trunk and is merely a rather clever play on words. Its simple meaning is that you need something as large as an elephant to consume such a large quantity – or eat a tun!

***

Today, with the benefit of affordable travel to exotic locations and the wide range of nature documentaries on television, we are familiar with wild animals from across the globe. However, in the nineteenth century the only way most people would be able to experience such wild beasts was by visiting travelling shows such as the famous Wombwell's Menagerie. This large collection of animals included elephants, llamas, gnus, tigers, lions, zebras, polar bears, ostriches and pelicans, which were transported around the country in wagons accompanied by a brass band.

The *Norfolk Chronicle* of 4 January 1840 reported:

> This splendid menagerie has, since our last notice of its arrival in Norwich, been visited by crowds of all ranks and ages. It certainly affords a very great treat as well to the intelligently curious as to the more careless or less informed observer to see so many noble and interesting specimens of remarkable animals.

Fair Green, in Diss, was visited regularly by travelling menageries and circuses in the 1800s, and local schoolchildren would flock to see these exotic animals. On 15 October 1867, however, tragedy struck during such a tour when the animals were being paraded along Denmark Street. The *Norfolk News* takes up the story:

> On Saturday 12th October 1867, Edmonds' Menagerie visited the town. On Monday morning Madame Abdella, a fine 20-year-old Burmese Elephant, refused to get up and move. Pulleys and tackle were used to put the animal onto a caravan, which returned to Fair Green. Cordials were administered, but on Tuesday she died. She was valued at £800–£900. She had been somewhat capricious and sulky of late, and only two weeks before had broken the arm of her keeper. Two men from London skinned the defunct elephant on Wednesday afternoon. As might be expected, considerable excitement was caused in the town.

It is believed that Madame Abdella was buried (or cremated and her remains buried or scattered) on Fair Green.

It is also strongly suspected that another elephant was interred beneath the same common ground. In 2019, a team with ground-penetrating radar found subterranean patterns that support the claim that an elephant is, indeed, buried there. One man who lived in Fair Green as a child recalls an incident that occurred in the mid-1940s. He remembers watching the carcass of an elephant being covered with a white powder, which was most probably quick lime. This substance helps speed up the decaying process and so could well have been used before burying the poor circus animal. So, one day perhaps, the skeleton of a descendent of the West Runton mammoth may be found in Diss!

★★★

Finally, while there are probably quite a few Norfolk residents who have lived to be around 100 years old, here are two examples from the nineteenth century. In the churchyard at Reedham there are graves to at least three centenarians.

One of these was Richard Pottle, who died in 1820 aged 108. He is remembered in the village by a road, Pottles Lane, which was named after their remarkable parishioner.

Over in Ashill, Reverend Bartholomew Edwards died in 1889, just a week or so short of his 100th birthday, while still holding the post of Rector of St Nicholas' Church. In fact, he notched up no less than seventy-six years' service as leader of the faithful in Ashill. His death was reported widely in the press up and down the country, including in the *Truth* newspaper, which wrote:

> The Rev. Bartholomew Edwards, Rector of Ashill, who died last week, was by far the oldest clergyman in England, having been born in 1789, and he was in many respects a most remarkable man. He lived a regular and extremely temperate life, and though a great diner-out, he was very sparing in the use of the good things of the table. Up to a great age he was a fine horseman, and took a great deal of exercise in that way, but he never rode to hounds. At all times, he indignantly declined to be helped on or off with his overcoat, and he never indulged in spectacles, saying that 'once they were used, there was no leaving them off'.

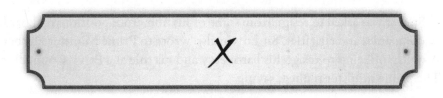

XENOPHOBIA

In the twentieth century, the chic coastal community of Overstrand earned a reputation for being the village of millionaires. One of the many fine houses, the Grange, was built for Sir John Hare, the actor-manager of London's Garrick Theatre. Then, in 1910, it was purchased by William Player of the tobacco company and, after him, by the founder of Boots the Chemist, Sir Jesse Boot.

For some time, Henry Royce, of Rolls-Royce, lived in a house called Pump Cottage in Overstrand. Another wealthy resident was Sir Edwin Speyer, who had the Edwardian mansion, Sea Marge, built on the clifftops above the beach. Speyer was an American-born financier and philanthropist of German parentage. He was also chairman of the Underground Electric Railways Company of London, a forerunner of the London Underground.

A rather less-known fact about Sir Edwin is that he is credited with having saved the annual Promenade Concerts in London. When Robert Newman, the manager of the Queen's Hall and founder of the Proms, was declared bankrupt in 1902, Speyer stepped in and reconstituted the resident orchestra as a limited company with himself as chairman. He subsidised the Proms from his own pocket, professionalised the orchestra and broadened its repertoire, championing new composers such as Edward Elgar and Claude Debussy.

The banker also acted as honorary treasurer of the fundraising committee for Captain Robert Falcon Scott's ill-fated expedition to the Antarctic. In fact, one of the twelve farewell letters Scott wrote in March 1912, when he realised that he and his team would not survive, was addressed to 'My dear Sir Edgar'.

Following the outbreak of the First World War there was inevitably widespread suspicion in Britain of people of German descent and it did not take long before rumours started to circulate that suggested Sir Edwin Speyer was allowing his house to be used as a signalling point for German submarines. The stories even reached the press and resulted in Speyer's rapid fall from grace.

Speyer was asked to resign from some of his numerous positions on boards of companies and charities. Sir Edwin also wrote to Prime Minister Herbert Asquith, offering to resign his baronetcy and his role as a Privy Councillor. The prime minister replied, saying:

> I have known you long, and well enough to estimate at their true value these baseless and malignant imputations upon your loyalty to the British Crown. The King is not prepared to take any step such as you suggest in regard to the marks of distinction which you have received in recognition of public services and philanthropic munificence.

Nevertheless, Sir Edwin Speyer had no choice but to move his family away from such controversy. They were driven into exile in the United States in 1915.

★★★

For several years in the lead-up to the outbreak of the First World War, people in Britain were gripped with fear of an invasion by the Germans. This paranoia was further fuelled in 1906 with the publication of *The Invasion of 1910*, a novel by William Le Queux. In it, German forces land in force on the east coast of England.

Encouraged by the huge success of this xenophobic, anti-German invasion fantasy, Le Queux wrote the espionage novel *Spies of the Kaiser*, in which Norfolk features significantly. There are German spies at work in north Norfolk coastal towns, such as Sheringham, and there is a dramatic car chase in pursuit of enemy agents through Wymondham, featuring places such as Aylsham, North Walsham and Cromer.

Little wonder, then, that when war was declared in August 1914, shops and businesses with German-sounding names were targeted by vandals. Pubs like the King of Prussia in Ipswich Road, Norwich, had their signs torn down.

The Defence of the Realm (Consolidation) Act allowed for all German citizens to be rounded up and incarcerated for the duration of the conflict. One notable incident occurred at the Hotel de Paris on the seafront at Cromer. Because members of the German royal family had stayed in the hotel before the war, a number of German waiters were employed there. Soldiers from the Essex Regiment who were billeted nearby arrested the waiters at gunpoint and transported them to Norwich. There, they were made to stand inside a ring of barbed wire and wood in the Market Place, guarded by the soldiers wielding their bayonets.

Cromer's iconic pier is overlooked by the Hotel de Paris. (Tony Scheuregger)

★★★

In 2005, a blue plaque was unveiled in Roughton, near Cromer, which marks a brief stay in the village by one of the most famous physicists in the world. In 1933, to escape Nazi persecution and death threats in Belgium, Albert Einstein was a guest of a British naval officer, Commander Oliver Locker-Lampson. Locker-Lampson's father had built Newhaven Court in Cromer and the house had played host to several eminent visitors, including Oscar Wilde, Lord Tennyson and Sir Ernest Shackleton.

Einstein was put up in a wooden cabin on Roughton Heath on land owned by the commander. Despite the modest accommodation, Albert was given access to luxuries such as a piano and violin. As well as being guarded by Locker-Lampson's armed staff, Einstein was provided with a butler to cook and serve him food. While in the hut, Albert Einstein continued to work and was even visited by the sculptor, Jacob Epstein, who completed a bust of the scientist during three separate sittings. It was common knowledge among residents that there was a genius in their midst and Einstein told a local newspaper reporter, 'All I want is peace, and could I have found a more peaceful retreat than here in England?'

YELLOW

Norwich City Football Club can trace its origins back to a meeting on 17 June 1902 at the Criterion Café in Norwich. The first nickname they adopted was the Citizens, but in 1907 this was changed to the Canaries.

The Norwich tradition of breeding canaries was introduced by the sixteenth-century Flemish settlers. The celebrated Norwich plainhead canary was one of the first varieties to be developed in England. It was bred and sold as far away as London and the bird's clear orange-yellow colour is thought to have come from feeding the birds cayenne pepper during moulting.

When the first recorded canary show was held on 16 November 1846 at the Greyhound Inn in Ber Street, the Norwich canary was the leading exhibition variety. Although it has now been surpassed by the Border canary and the Fife canary, the Norwich canary, which is larger and fatter than its nineteenth-century predecessors, is still exhibited in large numbers. It is bred for its physical appearance rather than for its colour or song. According to breeders, the Norwich or John Bull canary, as it is often known, make good pets because of their laid-back personalities!

★★★

The name Colman's and Norwich are synonymous to most people across the country. It is therefore sad that the last jar of the firm's iconic yellow mustard rolled off the production line in July 2019 to be followed shortly afterwards by its employees.

J. & J. Colman started life as a milling firm in the nearby village of Stoke Holy Cross. There, Jeremiah Colman took over a fledgling mustard business in 1814, improving the quality of production and machinery. In the late 1850s, Colman moved his business to a site in Carrow, Norwich, which was convenient for both river and rail transportation. It received a Royal Warrant in 1866 to supply mustard to Queen Victoria.

The firm grew rapidly until, by 1900, it had around 2,500 employees. The family business became known for the welfare they offered to their workers. A school was set up for children of employees and the company employed a staff nurse. After taking over rival mustard-maker Keen Robinson & Co. in 1903, Colman's also increased its standing by inventing Robinson's Barley Water, originally used to refresh and hydrate tennis players at the Wimbledon Championships.

On 9 November 1923, Ethel Colman, second daughter of Jeremiah Colman, was appointed the first Lady Lord Mayor of Norwich – also the first female lord mayor anywhere in England. Her lady mayoress was her sister, Helen Caroline Colman. During Ethel Colman's year in office, the Norfolk & Norwich Festival was revived, having been suspended since the start of the First World War.

Together, Ethel and Helen had the pleasure wherry *Hathor* built in memory of their brother, Alan, who had died in 1897 on a boat of the same name while convalescing in Luxor, Egypt. The interior of the vessel was designed by the renowned architect Edward Boardman.

In 1913, the sisters paid for the construction of a block of twenty-two flats to rehouse some of those affected by the great flood of 1912. Stuart Court, as it was called, was a memorial to their brother-in-law James Stuart (husband to their eldest sister, Laura) and is still used for low-income housing for the elderly.

On Laura's death in 1920, Ethel and Helen bought a fourteenth-century merchant's house in Norwich, called Suckling Hall, in their sister's memory. They had the house converted for use as a hall and cinema, again using Edward Boardman as architect for the project. Now renamed Stuart Hall, it was presented by the sisters to the city of Norwich in 1925 and remains in use today as a cinema.

Colman's advertising posters appealed to young and old alike.

ZEPPELINS

Before the twentieth century, the civilian population of Britain had been largely unaffected by war. Overseas wars rarely touched our shores, but the First World War changed all that, with the advent of war from the skies.

The eastern counties were particularly vulnerable to air attacks by the dreaded Zeppelin airships. These had been designed and developed by Count von Zeppelin in 1900 as a comfortable craft for passenger air travel. Soon afterwards seized on by the German military as potential weapons of war, these 190m-long hydrogen-filled, rugby-ball-shaped balloons soon became objects that struck fear into the British people. They could travel at about 85mph and carry up to 2 tonnes of bombs.

In the spring of 1909, British newspapers were reporting successful distance trials of the German Zeppelins and it was not long before accounts of unexplained airships over the country started to emerge. The first published sighting over Norfolk was made by a farm labourer at Terrington Marsh near King's Lynn. The *Daily Express* reported a statement by the labourer in which he described:

> … a whirring noise overhead, and when I look up I saw the fields round were lit up by a bright light. I was startled and wondered whatever could it be. Then I saw that the light came from a long, dark airship which was travelling swiftly overhead. It was low down – only a little way above the trees – so I could see it plainly. it seemed to be 80 or 100 feet long, and I could distinguish two men on a kind of hanging platform below.

Other sightings over the region swiftly followed, including over Sandringham, where the royal servants had spotted it.

It appears that either the mystery airships stopped visiting or the press had begun to tire of reporting the stories because the reports dried up later that year. There was then another spate of sightings in 1912, including over Hunstanton, and some more in 1913.

It was on the night of 18 January 1915 that the first German air raid on a civilian target in Britain was carried out. The first bombs to be dropped on British soil were on the north coast at Sheringham. The first to land, having failed to explode, was picked up by a local resident and put in a bucket.

Bombs were also dropped on the parish church at Snettisham, where a meeting had just finished. This action blew out some of the windows of the church but caused no casualties.

It was in Great Yarmouth, though, that the first ever British casualties of a Zeppelin air raid were recorded, with two residents losing their lives and two others sustaining injuries.

★★★

In the twentieth century, two large firms dominated the manufacturing sector in Norwich. One of these had its origins in an ironmonger's shop in London Street, then called Cockey Lane, in 1797. From these small beginnings grew the firm of Bouton & Paul. In the 1860s, the company opened a small factory in Rose Lane that, over the next century, was expanded. They produced a wide range of goods from wire netting and kitchen ranges to mincing and sausage-making machinery. As well as ironmongery, they also manufactured products from wood, including prefabricated huts and churches. In 1910, Boulton & Paul built the sledges used by Captain Robert Falcon Scott on his ill-fated expedition to the Antarctic.

The First World War, which had begun with cancellation of orders, proved highly profitable for Boulton & Paul. In 1915, they were asked to make aeroplanes and during the war the company produced 1,550 Sopwith Camels along with other types of aircraft. They made 2,530 military planes and supplied over 5,000 miles of the wire that was used to defend the British trenches.

At the end of the war, Boulton & Paul continued to make light metal aircraft for the Royal Air Force, as well as flying boat hulls for the navy. It was also in the 1920s that the firm made all the component parts – steel girders, cables, nuts and bolts – of the R101, an experimental passenger airship. These components were transported to the Royal Airship Works at Cardington in Bedfordshire where the R101 was assembled.

The ill-fated R101 airship, which crashed on its maiden overseas voyage.

Airship R101 made its first flight on 14 October 1929, when it made a short circuit over Bedford and London. Its third flight, lasting seven hours and fifteen minutes, was made on 1 November that year, during which it was flown at full power for the first time. On this flight it circled over Sandringham House, observed by George V and Queen Mary, flew on to Cromer, then to Norwich, over Boulton & Paul's works and aerodrome, before returning to Bedford via Newmarket and Cambridge.

A year later, the R101 crashed in France during its maiden overseas voyage, killing forty-eight of the fifty-four people on board, including the air minister who had initiated the programme, Lord Thomson. The crash of the R101 effectively ended British airship development.

Bibliography

Amyot, T.E., *Verses and Ballads* (Norwich: Agas H. Goose, 1897).

Brooks, P., *Norfolk Ghosts & Legends* (Wellington: Halsgrove, 2008).

Browning, S., and D. Tink, *Visitors' Historic Britain: Norwich and Norfolk: Bronze Age to Victorians* (Barnsley: Pen & Sword History, 2020).

Christian, C., *Shuckland: Weird Tales, Ghosts, Folklore and Legends from East Anglia's Waveney Valley* (Grantham: Heart of Albion Press, 2021).

Davies, J.A., *The Little History of Norfolk* (Cheltenham: The History Press, 2020).

Davies, J.A., and T. Pestell, *A History of Norfolk in 100 Objects* (Stroud: The History Press, 2012).

Davison, A., *Norfolk Origins Vol. 5: Deserted Villages in Norfolk* (North Walsham: Poppyland Publishing, 1996).

Doig, S.E., *Norwich at Work: People and Industries Through the Years* (Stroud: Amberley Publishing, 2020).

Evans, N., *A Collection of Diss History: Part 2* (Diss: Diss Museum Trustees, 1998).

Goodrum, P., *50 Gems of Norfolk: The History & Heritage of the Most Iconic Places* (Stroud: Amberley Publishing, 2017).

Hart, S., *The Round Church Towers of England* (Ipswich: Lucas Books, 2003).

Lupton, H., *Norfolk Folk Tales* (Stroud: The History Press, 2013).

McKenzie, R., *Ghost Fields of Norfolk: Histories, Plans & Photographed Remains of 32 Norfolk Airfields* (Dereham: The Larks Press, 2004).

Pursehouse, E., *Waveney Valley Studies: Gleanings from Local History* (Diss: Diss Publishing, 1983).

Puttick, B., *Norfolk Stories of the Supernatural* (Newbury: Countryside Books, 2010).

Skipper, K., *Hidden Norfolk* (Newbury: Countryside Books, 1998).

Storey, N.R., *A Grim Almanac of Norfolk* (Stroud: The History Press, 2010).

Storey, N.R., *Norfolk Murders* (Stroud: Sutton Publishing, 2006).

Storey, N.R., *Norfolk Tales of Mystery and Murder* (Newbury: Countryside Books, 2009).

Storey, N.R., *Norfolk Villains: Rogues, Rascals and Reprobates* (Stroud: The History Press, 2012).

Storey, N.R., *The Little Book of Norfolk* (Stroud: The History Press, 2011).

WEBSITES

The following websites used in researching this book were accessible at the time of writing between November 2022 and January 2023. Where I used Wikipedia website entries, I used fully sourced material or ensured that I verified details with at least one further source.

en.wikipedia.org
www.bbc.co.uk/news
www.british-history.ac.uk
www.broadlandmemories.co.uk
www.edp24.co.uk
www.fairgreendiss.wordpress.com
www.findmypast.co.uk
www.flht.co.uk
www.heritage.norfolk.gov.uk
www.holkham.co.uk
www.literarynorfolk.co.uk
www.lockhatters.com
www.nationaltrust.org.uk
www.norfolkchurches.co.uk
www.norfolktalesmyths.com
www.norfolkwildlifetrust.org.uk
www.ranworthchurch.com
www.roundtowers.org.uk
www.scase.co.uk/snailracing/
www.sirthomasbrowne.org.uk
www.spectator.co.uk
www.thenorwichsociety.org.uk
www.theoldie.co.uk
www.thewalks.uk
www.visitnorfolk.co.uk
www.visitnorthnorfolk.com

PERIODICALS

I consulted a large number of articles from the following periodicals, which are too numerous to list in full. Many of these provided invaluable inspiration for further research that resulted in the stories I feature in this book. I also made extensive use of old newspapers available via subscription on www.findmypast.co.uk.

East Anglian Magazine (*East Anglian Magazine* Ltd).
The Norfolk Ancestor (Norfolk Family History Society).
The Norfolk Magazine (The Norfolk Magazine).

The History Press — The destination for history — www.thehistorypress.co.uk